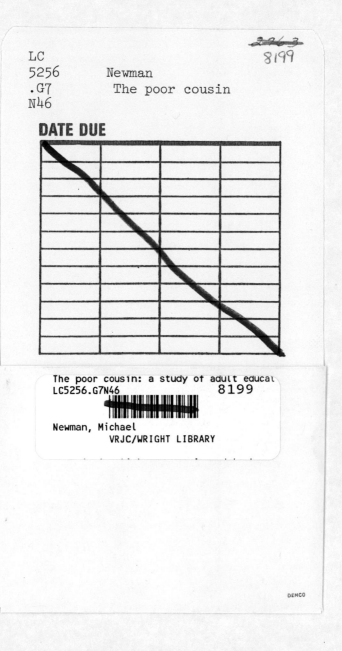

THE POOR COUSIN
A study of adult education

By the same author

Adult Education and Community Action (Writers and
    Readers Publishing Cooperative, 1975)

THE
POOR COUSIN

A Study of Adult Education

by MICHAEL NEWMAN

London
GEORGE ALLEN & UNWIN
Boston   Sydney

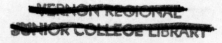

First published in 1979

GEORGE ALLEN & UNWIN LTD
40 Museum Street, London WC1A 1LU

© Michael Newman, 1979

British Library Cataloguing in Publication Data

Newman, Michael
    The poor cousin.
    1. Adult education—Great Britain
    I. Title
    374.9'41   LC5256.G7   78-40740

    ISBN 0-04-374002-2

Typeset in 11 on 12 point Baskerville by Red Lion Setters and printed in Great Britain
by Biddles Ltd, Guildford, Surrey.

Contents

x *Contents*

PART IV *Survival Learning*

Preface

At the outset I would like to make four points. The first is that this is a personal book, starting from and returning to my own experiences in adult education. It is the method I have chosen of approaching a very diverse subject but it has not stopped me from drawing general conclusions; and it is my hope that by the end of the book the reader will agree that many of these conclusions can apply to the education of adults in a wide range of contexts.

The second point follows from the first. Throughout the book I keep returning to the activities of one particular adult education centre, but I most certainly do not want to create the impression that adult education only occurs in isolated places or in one type of institution. Every year between 2½m and 3m adults in the UK enrol in tens of thousands of adult education classes sponsored by a wide range of statutory and voluntary agencies employing more than 100,000 part-time tutors. Adult education is spread wide.

The third point is directed at a particular group of people. There is a move amongst some adult educators to 'professionalise' the service. There is much talk about training in order to rid the service of its 'amateur' image. There are even some who suggest that adult education should not employ tutors unless they are teacher-trained. These adult educators may find much in the book to disagree with, but it is my hope that they will still find my ideas worth discussing. The debate between the advocates of 'professionalism' and those who want adult education to retain and develop the best of its 'amateur' attributes is a crucial one.

And the fourth point is a formality. At the time of writing I was employed by the Inner London Education Authority, which permitted much of what is described in this book to take place. However the views expressed are mine and obviously ILEA accepts no responsibility for my opinions and conclusions.

PART I

'We are a centre for leisure learning and we operate in your area'

Chapter 1

The Poor Cousin

Adult education is the poorest and often the most neglected sector of the education service and for the most part this book will take this statement as read. But since my aim is to describe the colour, variety and adventure available in adult education and to argue that adult education is often in the vanguard of educational experimentation, perhaps it would be wise at the outset to underline just how poor the poor cousin is.

For a start, the law is a little foggy on adult education. The 1944 Education Act, while being quite specific on the duties of local education authorities to provide primary, secondary and further education, actually fails to mention *adult* education by name. Instead it includes what is generally understood as adult education under the blanket title of 'further education' along with a lot of educational activity that has nothing at all to do with adult education. And while local authorities, it would seem, have a duty under the Act to provide further education, apparently that duty does not extend to adult education. The *Russell Report* (1973)[1] comes to this slightly nonplussed conclusion:

> We are advised, therefore, that while it may have been surprising, it was not in the circumstances unlawful for one or two local authorities in 1968 to propose as a measure of economy to suspend their adult education altogether, including their support of other providing agencies.
>
> (para. 158)

In other words local authorities are encouraged to provide

adult education, but when the chips are down they do not actually have to do so. And to make matters worse this lack of clear statutory commitment has been accompanied by what the *Russell Report* notes drily as 'the limited extent of the leadership from central government in the development of adult education in this country' (para. 155). Most of the initiatives from central government, the report continues, have usually had the raising of fees as their primary concern.

Local authorities quite naturally therefore tend to put adult education low on their list of priorities, to be provided with what finance, energy and enthusiasm are left after all the statutory requirements of the other sectors have been met. Adult education remains vulnerable at times of financial stringency. One local authority ordered a cut of 47 per cent in its adult education teaching costs from 1975-6 to 1976-7. Another reduced its adult education year from thirty-five weeks to thirty from one year to the next, and planned a drop to twenty-six weeks for the following year. And yet any savings achieved by such cutbacks can be seen as minuscule when one realises that barely 1 per cent of the total expenditure of local authorities goes to adult education in the first place.[2] Of course conditions vary from authority to authority—from the authorities alluded to in the *Russell Report* above, to the Inner London Education Authority (ILEA), which provides a network of thirty adult education institutes and three literary institutes attended by over a quarter of a million adults, as well as providing financial support for a large number of other agencies. Yet even here the expenditure on adult education— nearly 3 per cent of ILEA's total revenue expenditure in 1976-7 and more than twice the national average[3]—remains marginal.

Brackenbury

Perhaps the best way of making the point is to go in and take a look at a centre.

This is all too often easier said than done. Take, for example, the Brackenbury branch of Addison Adult Education Institute in West London. It is a forbidding Victorian school building, surrounded by high brick walls and chicken wire.

Having in all likelihood made a false start through some double gates or down a side lane into a taxi depot, you enter a narrow hole in the wall and wander across an ill-lit patch of asphalt. Here you have a choice between a normal-sized door on your right, leading into the schoolkeeper's house, and the door into the main building on the left which through some quirk of relative proportions, appears oddly undersize. The door on the left it is, but once into the building the only obvious path is up a set of bare concrete stairs, the walls lined with tiles, leading you wandering into a box room used by the photography group as a dark room, or into a section of the building rarely used in the evenings. What you must know, since there is often no sign to indicate it, is that the door to the right at the foot of the staircase that looks like a cupboard in fact opens into a narrow corridor which leads into the heart of the building.

Here quite suddenly you are greeted by the sight of the central hall filled with ballroom dancers (in mufti) moving in complex patterns to the muted shouts of the dance instructor. To the right off this central hall is an arts and crafts class, across the hall on the other side of the building are two classes in English as a second language, to the left is the canteen, and to the left and left again is a painting class; upstairs are a literacy group, a domestic electricity class, and the photography class spread between the dark room and another room set up with lights as a portrait studio; while across the playground in two small annexes are classes in upholstery, woodwork, dressmaking and car maintenance. And once you have actually found where it is all happening you will note that the place is warm, busy and friendly.

But the building is shared with a primary school and the electricity class are sitting on infants' furniture. The ballroom dancers are dancing to decidedly tinny music issuing from a light portable record-player perched carefully on a table so as not to disturb the children's art display. The painting class have positioned their easels in whatever space has been left in their classroom by the 'open plan' arrangement of day-school furniture so that the tutor, a large Scot, is obliged to squeeze between a variety of obstacles on his round of his students, taking care not to knock over the reading nook, disturb the guinea pigs or send a fish tank crashing to the floor. Out in the annexes the dressmakers are not very well heated and the car maintenance people have to be inordinately careful about pools of oil because their indoor discussion room doubles as a crèche attached to a small number of classes held in the annexe during the day and their outdoor space is part of the children's playground. On closer inspection the canteen proves to be a classroom converted for the evening by the provision of a hot-water urn in one corner. The administrative staff work in the corridor at a table and the easels, the gramophone and any adult-sized furniture have to be packed away in a storeroom at the end of each evening. And that lack of signposting comes about because children can often remove signs put up by the evening lot, so after a while the evening lot stop putting them up.

Certainly there are a number of purpose-built adult education centres. Nothing could be further from Brackenbury in standard of accommodation than the brand new headquarters of the Sutton College of Liberal Arts, with its fully equipped gymnasium, its drama and video studio, its purpose-built craft rooms, its tiered lecture theatre and its cafeteria and licensed bar. Certainly there are a number of leisure complexes or community schools with provision for adult education included in the original design, and there are a number of buildings, mostly former schools, that have been re-equipped solely for adult use. But these are exceptions and Brackenbury remains the rule. Adult education operates on a shoestring, in makeshift conditions, and on somebody else's premises.

Chapter 2

An Adult Education Centre

Non-definition
The trouble with talking about adult education is that it is not
a single concept. The *Russell Report* puts it this way:

> In practice, and in terms of the Education Act 1944, there is
> a spectrum called further education which at one end is
> clearly vocational (though still not unconnected with per-
> sonal and social development) and at the other is personal,
> social, cultural and non-vocational. (para. 4)

The report says that adult education is to be found along at
the personal, social, cultural and non-vocational end but is
quick to add that it sees no virtue in drawing 'a sharp line of
division' across the spectrum at any one particular point. It
does state quite clearly, however, that in talking about adult
education it excludes 'the major areas of higher, technical and
art education'.

And to unnerve the meticulously minded further, adult
education is not provided by a single, easily identifiable,
agency or even one type of agency. The providers include the
local education authorities, the Workers' Educational Association (WEA), the universities through their extramural departments, the settlements and all manner of other organisations
ranging from the churches, to industry, to local clubs.[4] And
even the way in which the main providers, the local
authorities, go about their jobs varies enormously from place
to place.

Yet similarities do exist in the activities these various

agencies provide. The phrase 'adult education' *does* have a meaning. And adult education can be seen to operate according to a number of principles that are common to most of its activities and very different from those in operation in other sectors of the education service.

However, before I can demonstrate this I need to set the scene; and rather than start with a survey of all the providers, an impossible task in any event, I want to describe one adult education centre and work from there.

A Leaflet

The Brackenbury branch I have described is part of the Addison Institute, and in the first week of January 1976 Addison organised a 24,000 leaflet drop in the area the institute serves. The leaflet carried information on courses and activities available at the institute's main branches. On the front was an explanatory statement. These were the first two paragraphs:

We are a centre for leisure learning and we operate in your area. Our job is to provide you with the facilities, equipment and tuition by experts to help you develop your interests or hobbies.

We run over 500 classes a week in over 80 different subjects. Our students come from all walks of life and age groups. The atmosphere is friendly and relaxed and everyone sets their own pace. There are no exams.

The Area

The area referred to is roughly the northern half of the London Borough of Hammersmith. It includes the old London districts of West Kensington, Hammersmith, Shepherd's Bush, White City, Wormwood Scrubs and College Park, and has everything you could want (or not want) in an inner city area. It has Hammersmith Broadway and Shepherd's Bush Green, two of the busiest roundabouts in the country. It has Wormwood Scrubs Prison, Olympia Exhibition Hall, White City Stadium, Queen's Park Rangers Football Ground and the BBC Television Centre. It has the enormous bleak expanse of Wormwood Scrubs with a tangle of railway lines and a canal running

across the north of it. Its eastern boundary is marked by a
railway line and the part-constructed, part-aborted inner
motorway box, leading all of half a mile from a roundabout to
its massive elevated junction with Westway. The area has a lot
of Victorian housing, some post-war, gap-filling constructions,
four tower blocks on the south side of Shepherd's Bush Green
and a number of large housing estates including White City. It
has the river to the south-western side. It has some small but
often pleasant greens and parks. It has a lot of pubs, some with
strippers, one with a celebrated drag act and gay disco, many
with not very good music, and one with excellent folk music;
and another with a leading fringe theatre in a room upstairs. It
has a newly opened arts centre by the river, a modern theatre,
six cinemas, (one of them doubling up as one of London's
main venues for rock concerts) and two large bingo halls. It
has the Hammersmith flyover, and the Hammersmith Palais.
It has lots of churches, two tabernacles, a synagogue, and a
temple. It has a large commercial laundry, a range of small
factories and workshops and the home offices of at least two
very large national companies. It has two main shopping
areas, one doing quite well and incorporating Shepherd's Bush
Market alongside and under the arches of the elevated
Metropolitan line, the other in King Street savaged almost
out of existence by extensive re-development. The area has
innumerable cafés and not many trendy wine bars or restaurants. It has a lot of small hotels and rooming houses,
one massive international hotel and a crash pad for the single
homeless.

According to the 1971 census, 88,450 people live in the
northern half of the borough. There are 19,950 children aged
sixteen and under, proportionately fewer than in the rest of the
country, and there are 14,600 people of pensionable age,
proportionately more than in the rest of the country.

It is a multiracial area. According to the 1971 census, 28 per
cent of the population were born outside the UK. The English
are there, of course—posh ones in the villagey areas around
Brook Green and by the river, trendies in the bijou converted
workers' cottages behind Olympia, that newly oppressed class
known as the mansion block dweller in splendid mansion
blocks and some seedy ones along and to the south of

Hammersmith Road, young middle-class couples near Ravenscourt Park, working class all round the Bush, up in College Park, in White City, spread pretty well everywhere, in fact, and apart from one or two pockets not yet grossly outnumbered. There are lots of Irish and lots of people with Irish parents. A lot of West Indians live in the area too—the tropical vegetables in the market and the thump of reggae from the record shops tell you they have settled in—round Askew Road and Conningham Road particularly, but spread pretty widely elsewhere. There are Asian Asians—there's a Chinese centre in the basement of a Methodist church—and Asians from East Africa. There are West Africans too, and Cypriots and Spaniards and Italians and a Frenchman or two and Arabs, a group of whom are sometimes to be seen after market with their veiled and silent women folk waiting in Goldhawk Road just outside Cooke's pie and eel shop. There is a large modern Polish cultural and social centre in King Street. And in West Kensington there is a fluid population of people from the English provinces, the Commonwealth, the Americas and everywhere else in the world, all sharing that rootless, classless life-style common to occupants of bed-sitters.

And to round off this very incomplete sketch, the area has six London Underground stations, three London Transport bus garages, four branch libraries, three major hospitals, two large police stations, a hostel for the mentally handicapped, two colleges, seven secondary and any number of primary schools, an old folk's home, a busy employment exchange, a detention centre for young offenders, and most of the other standard civic amenities including, as the leaflet announced, Addison Adult Education Institute.

Premises

Adult education centres come in all shapes and sizes, based on whatever accommodation they have been given or have managed to scrounge, and developing in various directions according to the dictates of their areas and their resources and the particular interests and eccentricities of their heads of centre. A centre in North Kensington in London has a branch almost entirely devoted to body-building, wrestling and weight-lifting—furnitureless classrooms with dumb-bells and exercising equipment lying about on bare floorboards. Why this branch in this particular centre? Another centre has a branch on a ship moored on a river. Some 'centres' may have no centre at all but consist of a scatter of classes, sponsored by the WEA together with a university, say, and housed in clubs, community centres and church halls in a number of villages dotted round a market town.

That being said, however, Addison does fit into a recognisable category. It is a middling to large local authority centre, operating in an urban area and enjoying a reasonable amount of autonomy. It is one of thirty similar ILEA institutes. It has five main branches. Its headquarters are on the top floor of a primary school. On this one floor Addison has a permanent canteen, a hall, and various specialist rooms—or rather, various schoolrooms converted into a pottery studio (squeezed into the attic), a dressmaking room, two arts and crafts rooms, a language room, a liberal studies room and a 'lecture room'. Into this space, by the ingenious use of partitions and the simple expedient of overcrowding, are also fitted the administrative staff together with the stock and a lot of the equipment for the whole institute. The institute also has a woodwork room, a combination car-maintenance/upholstery room (piston rings kept apart from velvet coverings by yet another partition) and part use of a science room in two annexes in the playground. The institute runs classes on the top floor and in the annexes during the day and in the evenings moves downstairs to take over the primary area as well.

The other main branches are schools during the day—two secondary, two primary—which at six o'clock each evening become part of the institute. In addition Addison uses two other schools one evening a week each, a privately owned building for a limited programme of courses four days a week, and a number of halls and rooms dotted about the area where it supports day and evening activities in conjunction with local organisations and welfare services.

Programme
As the leaflet said, Addison runs more than 500 classes a week.

A class is normally a two-hour meeting once a week, so that in adult education parlance 'intensive French' will mean that the group meets twice a week for a total, when one removes time for tea-breaks, of no more than three and a half hours' tuition. This must be carefully explained to enquiring businessmen. Addison provides these 500 classes a week for thirty-five weeks in the year, with some of the welfare classes running the whole year round.

But what sort of classes? To choose one subject from the list under each letter of the index in Addison's prospectus:

angling, brass band, continental cookery, drama, electronic workshop, fencing, guitar, home decoration, Italian, judo, keep fit, life drawing, music appreciation, old-time dancing, public speaking, Russian, sculpture, table tennis, upholstery, volley ball, writers' workshop, and yoga.

In the body of the prospectus the eighty or so subjects are grouped under the following headings:

Community development and welfare classes; Special studies; Reading and writing; Languages; Fine art; Arts and crafts; Sports, pastimes and physical education; Acting, music and dance; Food and drink; Domestic crafts; and Technical subjects.

To teach this programme Addison employs more than 300 part-time tutors. Obviously, with so many premises and such a large part-time staff, administrative slip-ups can occur and the quality of tuition occasionally falls below standard; but year after year, with a minimum of fuss and to the manifest satisfaction of the students who would stop attending if they were not getting the goods, Addison provides a basic programme along the lines outlined above.

It is a programme of extraordinary scope. And it is all the more impressive when one realises that it is in no way unique to Addison, but that all the subjects and categories are reasonably regular fare at any of the other well-established adult education centres around the country.

Fees

The statement on the front of Addison's leaflet had this to say about fees:

> We are part of the Inner London Education Authority, and as ratepayers you have already paid most of the price of taking part. As a result enrolment fees are normally about £1 per term. There is a reduction for those students unable to pay the full fee.

Of course, in this day and age figures are never right for long. That £1 was £2 the following academic year, and £2.50 for 1977 - 8 with considerably less advantageous concessions if you joined more than one class. Nor are the ILEA fees representative of the scale of fees charged elsewhere. In fact fees for adult education vary enormously from authority to authority, ranging from the comparatively low fees ILEA charges to fees that are calculated to cover the full teaching cost of the course. But even then an adult education activity is still subsidised in the form of the accommodation and administration it has access to as a result of being part of the education service as a whole. The group is meeting in a school, watching slides on the school's projector and screen, using heating and lighting, being locked up after by the school's caretaking staff, all this being administered from town or county hall. And when the adult education activity is provided by an agency other than the local education authority, such as the WEA or a university department or a settlement, the agency is usually grant-aided — as often as not receiving some of its funds directly from the local education authority. So the situation stated in Addison's leaflet remains generally true. Adult education is one of the services we receive as ratepayers and as a result the fees are low.

Chapter 3

The Numbers Game

The Magic Number

Adult education depends in a starkly simple way on attendance. A class exists only so long as the required number of people attend. The magic number varies from authority to authority, agency to agency, and even sometimes from one subject area to another within the same centre, but is rarely less than ten and sometimes as high as twenty. If the initial enrolment does not reach this stipulated minimum the course does not start. And in the case of a course already under way, if the attendance drops off, so does the class. In most adult education prospectuses, somewhere in the small print, you will find this sort of reminder:

> The right is reserved to refuse admission to the institute, to close a class or to combine the class with another and to exclude any student.

Statements of this ilk are not made to cover the centre against remote eventualities. In adult education when we talk about class closures, class amalgamations and turning people away we mean what we say.

Of course there are cases where the strict application of the minimum attendance rule will be relaxed. Some centres are permitted by their overlords to treat the number as an average attendance for their whole programme, enabling them to balance the less well attended activities against the crowd pullers. Others will be permitted to exempt certain priority classes—music and movement for the handicapped, say—from the rule or at least to apply a lower minimum number to certain categories of classes. But even though relaxations to the rule may occasionally be permitted, the poor cousin is obliged to look to its numbers in a way that its more privileged relatives in the other sectors of the education service would not tolerate. This explains why adult educators welcome the local opera group with open arms, letting all seventy or eighty of them occupy the lower hall on Tuesdays and Fridays and bellow to their hearts' content. And it explains why, having done his homework on the inner workings of adult education, a Catholic priest approached a centre with the proposal that he and a fellow priest should run a course on Catholicism, saying: 'Before I explain anything else, I can guarantee you more than a hundred people a night'.

Heads of centre listen to this sort of suggestion because their centres are graded according to attendance and the number of classes, and if the numbers go up enough so does the grade, and so does the head's salary. It is called 'the numbers game'.

A Little Tick Here, a Little Tick There

Adult education's dependence on numbers can lead to certain anomalies and abuses. There is always the temptation to go for the crowd pullers without paying too much attention to the educational content. That opera group in all its mighty strength may well permit a centre to run several other classes that might otherwise go by the board, but does a 'student' attending rehearsals year in, year out, for the annual production — *Desert Song* this year, *The Mikado* last — actually learn anything?

And there is the temptation to go for numbers to the exclusion of quality, and pack forty people into a language class when to do the job competently, let alone well, the tutor should have no more than twenty. Or to go for numbers not only to the detriment of the class but so as physically to endanger the individual student. Certain yoga positions inexpertly performed can harm one's spine and neck and yet some centres may be tempted to over-enrol their yoga classes to such an extent that the tutor will be hard put to it to check the posture of every student with the rigour the discipline requires.

And then there are the registers. An adult education tutor

quickly realises that the survival of his class, and the extra pocket money he is earning by taking it, depend on his having the right number of people in the room . . . or, if he is not too closely supervised, marked down on his register.

The register may even become everything. Some years ago, so legend has it, a centre with several branches somewhere in the UK was split up and shared out between neighbouring centres. On paper the carved-up centre was a flourishing one but when the head of one of the neighbouring centres visited a newly acquired branch for the first time he was disturbed to find the building ablaze with lights yet powered by nothing more substantial than a set of neatly filled in registers. There were no people. Or at least very few. One version of the story says the head of centre found a boot-repairing class with one person in it — the tutor repairing his own boots!

Abuses are necessarily rare, however, in a service whose clients are articulate adults unlikely to tolerate their time being wasted or their rates being squandered. And the numbers game does have its advantages. It obliges the adult educator to pore over the attendance returns of all the activities of his centre, monitoring their fluctuations. To a limited extent at least it makes him aware of the shifting pattern of interests and aspirations in the surrounding community. And it obliges him to take these shifts into account, by increasing provision in some subjects, reducing it in others, closing ailing classes and setting up new ones. The numbers game keeps the adult educator on his toes, casting round for ideas for new courses that will 'go'. It makes him experiment.

Set-'em-up-and-see

The most common form of experiment is the set-'em-up-and-see method. A lot of adult education operates in this way because the poor cousin rarely has enough staff to experiment in any other way. As late as 1971, for example, Addison had only two full-time staff members. Since then there has been an increase, but in this respect London institutes have been lucky. In many parts of the country adult education centres still have very few full-time members of staff and in some cases are administered by a 'principal' whose duties are divided fifty-fifty between his centre and a school where he may also have a considerable daytime teaching load.

The set-'em-up-and-see method is exactly what it says. The adult educator sets up a few courses to fill the gaps left in his programme by those that have failed. If they go, good luck to the tutors and students involved. And if they do not go, he closes them down and tries again a little later with something else. The actual subjects introduced into a centre's programme in this way will depend on any number of things—the adult educator's current interests, obsessions and contacts; what existing members of the teaching staff might be able to offer; who have written in recently offering their services; a chance encounter . . . . Here, from The *Times* Diary, is how a course on reviewing the arts came into existence at one particular centre:[5]

> The idea of teaching the course was not mine. I had gone to the institute to sign on as a student for a language class. The head of the Humanities Department, who interviewed me, was a friend of a theatre director whose play I had reviewed favourably a short time before. Moreover two students had asked for a course in reviewing that very week.
>
> 'Go away and get together a course outline, love,' said the head, waving a denimed arm . . . .

The *Times* Diary introduces the critic's account as an 'unusual experience'. It may have been unusual for the critic but it was standard practice for adult education. The adult educator saw an opportunity for a course that might go, and seized it.

By using the set-'em-up-and-see method, adult education can be flexible and respond on the spur of the moment; but the method has a basic flaw. If courses are set up on the off-chance, then there is bound to be a high failure rate. The closure of classes will become a normal event at the centre, rather than one to be resisted. And the adult educator will find it all too easy to fall into the habit of killing off a course whose numbers are dropping rather than engage in the sometimes difficult and delicate task of finding out what is going wrong, and, where possible, correcting it.

Reasons for Failure

Not all adult education classes fail because of irredeemably bad teaching or because the subject has suddenly dropped out of fashion. They may fail because one tetchy old gentleman has soured the atmosphere. They may fail because the tutor does not join the group during tea-break. They may fail because the room is too stuffy, or badly lit, or the desks are the wrong size. They may fail because the tutor is good but inexperienced in handling a diverse group of adults. And of course they may fail through the ineptitude of the centre and through no fault of the class, the subject or the tutor.

There was the example of the 'Cartoon and Comic Strip Design' course at Addison. The course was intended as a practical art class with a maximum of sixteen students. Through some administrative slip-up, however, forty-two people were enrolled. These forty-two people were allocated a room with thirty individual desks with slanting desk-tops that could accommodate little more than a person's two elbows. The tutor was new to teaching—a professional cartoonist, in fact. He was not met by anyone from the institute, had to find the room himself, and without warning walked into a room filled with forty-two grimly silent adults. The tutor displays dismay in his eyes when recalling the first evening. He had intended to start straight into a practical exercise, but the room and the numbers made that impossible. He says he began talking, gabbling. He detected not one friendly face in the room, just a nightmarish sea of resentment stretching before him. No one told him there was a tea-break, so the tutor—he stammers slightly and dabs at his meaning in short, incomplete phrases in a way that shows he is not at ease with extended speech—spoke non-stop for two hours! Within two weeks the attendance had dropped below the minimum number. The course was not closed and the numbers built up again over the next few weeks, but if the numbers game had been strictly adhered to, that class would have lasted no more than a fortnight.

Public relations

The regular closure of classes is bad public relations. After all, it is seldom the fault of the student who enrols and continues attending that others do not enrol or fail to continue attending. Yet if the closure of classes is the accepted way of tidying up a centre's books then this blameless student finds his course suddenly, peremptorily cut off. The set-'em-up-and-see method is such established practice that many centres actually begin each year with more classes than their allocation of resources permits—thus wilfully intending to chop a certain percentage from their advertised programme. But once the people in the area know the centre is in the habit of closing classes, they will naturally tend to avoid the new or experimental course, knowing that its chances of running the distance are much slimmer than one of the regular fare. In this way the set-'em-up-and-see method actually works against itself.

In its extreme form the method does away with public relations altogether. The adult educator remains in his centre, setting up courses and poring over the attendance returns, feeling no need to consult with outsiders at all. His knowledge of the community remains limited to what is passively expressed through the attendance statistics, which in their turn are limited to that small part of the community that already makes use of the centre. The whole process becomes an exercise in educational and administrative masturbation.

Chapter 4
Image

By late 1973 Addison Institute's full-time staff had been increased to six, and the institute was able to review its programme more thoroughly. It was decided to try and develop the Brackenbury branch. The accommodation there was under-used, particularly one of the annexes in the playground. Although Addison had the use of this annexe both day and evening, the daytime programme consisted of no more than three or four dressmaking classes per week and one afternoon of tailoring. The annexe was small and scruffy; but with some reorganisation and the judicious introduction of a partition or two it would be possible to run two or three courses simultaneously both morning and afternoon, with a crèche attached. But what sort of classes? The institute decided to carry out a survey of the people in the area around Brackenbury and ask them. Now that it had the staff, Addison was going to adopt the very opposite of the set-'em-up-and-see method of programme design.

A questionnaire was drawn up and the full-time staff, two students from the planning department of Central London Polytechnic who offered to help, and several of the institute's part-time staff began knocking on the doors of the 800 houses and flats within roughly a quarter-mile radius of the branch.

One Street
I was one of the full-time staff and these are some of the people I interviewed in one street:

A young couple I was invited into their room. They were English-born blacks and both under twenty. I might not have realised they were a couple but for the very small baby in the midst of a nappy change, legs held high, at the moment I was ushered in. The one room with a gas ring in the corner was their entire home. They knew nothing about adult education or Brackenbury. The mother said the idea of dressmaking classes during the daytime sounded interesting, but it was a polite reply. If they were ever to get out of that room they would both have to find work, which made any talk of daytime classes irrelevant.

An elderly woman She was in her early seventies and lived alone in a single room overlooking the back garden of the house. She said she rarely went out. 'I like to sit here', she said. Yes, she knew something went on in the evenings at the school along at the end of the road but it did not concern her since it was only for the young. She seemed a little incredulous when I told her many people her age and older attended adult education activities.

A bus driver He was a middle-aged man and born and bred in the district. He knew that such things as evening classes existed and had often wondered whether he might not wander into the school at the end of the road and see what was going on there. We chatted affably until he glanced at his watch in mid-sentence and said: 'I'm off to work now'. It was four in the afternoon.

A redundant foreman packer He was a tall, thin Irishman dressed in a neat, light-grey suit. He invited me in for coffee and he and his attractive wife and I chatted in the kitchen of their flat. He was living on his savings but they had nearly gone. 'I haven't looked for work', he said. He thought he might try mini-cab driving. The conversation drifted aimlessly, never lighting on one subject for long, and I got the feeling that neither of them would want to subscribe to an activity that stretched thirty-five weeks into the future.

A mother of seven She reckoned cheerfully that she was never free from at least two of her children, and she was doubtful that a crèche could contain any of them. She said she knew all about dressmaking, was in no need of a keep-fit class and had no other suggestions for activities we might put on. A squalling noise from inside the house drew her away with the questionnaire still incomplete.

A shift worker I got no reply from any of the buttons in a multi-occupied house, so pushed them all again and was rewarded for my gross lack of consideration by a sharp lecture from a tough-looking West Indian of about thirty who told me he worked nights and I had just woken him. It was about two-thirty in the afternoon. 'I've just come in off the street, man,' he told me. 'You got to try me in the mornings.'

A musician I was invited into a flat occupied by four professional musicians all in their twenties — a guitarist, two saxophonists and a trombonist. No one seemed to follow the same routine. One was cooking himself bacon and eggs at four in the afternoon while others came and went from other rooms, other flats in the house, and the outside world. The phone rang several times while I was there. 'Couldn't do evening classes', the one who had invited me in told me. 'Never know where I am from one week to the next. Gig in Brighton, session in Birmingham, know what I mean?'

A middle-class housewife She was the only person I spoke to who appeared to own the house she lived in and she was the only person to react to the question: 'Do you know that if enough people want a course or a subject not already in our programme, we will do our best to put the course on?' 'Really?' she said. 'Does that mean that if I and some friends wanted a course on Chinese cookery, you could arrange it?'

I managed to interview fully eighteen people living in the street but spoke to many more than that; and it was only while going through the results after the event that I realised that not one person from the first four houses on the south side of the street, from whose front steps the Brackenbury branch was clearly visible, had any idea that evening classes took place in the building. One woman said that she had heard the brass band but had not stopped to wonder why the lights burned in the building on the other evenings as well.

The Addison Brackenbury Community Centre
The results of the survey were tabulated and discussed. People

had said they would like dressmaking, car maintenance and flower arranging, all subjects amply provided for in the existing programme. There were few other clues and certainly no blinding flash of light. The survey of the area had been accompanied by a questionnaire distributed to students already attending the branch and a reasonably extensive contact with local voluntary and statutory bodies, but these two exercises produced no more hard suggestions for activities in the annexe than the street interviews had. The next step was a public meeting, held jointly with the Grove Neighbourhood Council in whose area the school stood, at which the institute outlined the accommodation available and the plans so far, and called for discussion and suggestions. A limited pilot programme of daytime courses was then set up in third term; and in the following year, 1974-5, a programme of classes, four mornings and four afternoons a week with a crèche attached, was successfully launched in the annexe, now renamed — incorrectly — the Addison Brackenbury Community Centre.

By 1975-6 the subjects at the ABC Centre during the day included French, demonstration cookery, English for immigrants, fashion and design, tailoring, arts and crafts, Italian, dressmaking, upholstery, and literacy classes — all subjects the institute would most likely have put on had it gone blithely ahead with the set-'em-up-and-see method. The annexe, despite a flick of paint and a square of carpet here and there, was still a small, scruffy-looking outhouse down at the bottom of the playground. It was all a little makeshift, but it seemed to work.

Evaluation

So what value the survey? In terms of the branch and the annexe, not much. It had been of no real use in telling the institute what to put on. It had been of some use in making contacts — the woman who ran the crèche for the first year was first encountered as an interviewee. And in a limited way the survey had been a good publicity exercise, in that a couple of hundred more people knew of the existence of the institute simply because someone had knocked on their front doors and told them about it.

But in terms of the staff the effects of the survey were

far-reaching. It made us talk to people. It made us aware of the diversity and complexity of people's lives. It reminded us that the community we were there to serve consisted of more than the people we saw in the branches. It made us toss ideas around, and talk about adult education.

The survey also made us aware of the people the institute was failing to reach — the elderly, the housebound, the shift worker — and gave the lie to the numbers game. By studying the institute's existing programme, for example, it was easy to gain the impression that we were doing everything we could for the elderly. We already ran a not inconsiderable number of activities in day centres for the elderly, and many of our regular daytime and evening activities were patronised by people well over retirement age. Yet a surprising number of the elderly encountered during the survey were unaware of the programme we offered, or thought that it was all examination work aimed at the young. This distressing comment on our public relations indicated not only that many of the elderly themselves were ignorant of the role adult education could play in their lives, but that the people in contact with them — doctors, health visitors, social and community workers, the churches — were also unaware of the real character of adult education and failed to recommend us.

The survey also showed up disturbing limitations in the conventional adult education provision. There was nothing in our programme to make the shift worker insist that an activity be changed to a time that would suit him. There was nothing to make the housebound mother demand that we provide a crèche so that she could attend. The programme may have been varied and interesting, but it lacked pulling power. It lacked relevance. What, for example, did we really have to offer that young couple I interviewed? From all appearances they were having to struggle simply in order to survive, and here was someone asking them questions about a leisure learning programme that included floral art, lingerie, cake decoration, cinema appreciation and fly-tying!

That young couple might never have enough time to attend an adult education course, however much pull it had and no matter how relevant; but in recognition of their existence the institute could at least engage in activities that examined and sought solutions to the social and community ills of which they were victims. The survey was by no means the starting-point for this type of thinking—a shift in emphasis was already under way in adult education in several parts of the country—but it served very forcefully to underline the need to broaden the institute's programme and include courses for child minders, increase our literacy provision, try setting up 'mothers and babies' groups, experiment in length and approach and timing of existing courses, and provide courses on issues such as housing, environment, poverty and job opportunity as educational back-up to community development and action.

This shift in thinking and the problems it throws up are the subject of the third and fourth parts of the book; but the point brought home most clearly by the Brackenbury survey was that an alarming number of people did not know an adult education service existed at all, or thought it was something else.

Prejudices
The common prejudices one hears expressed about adult education are wildly conflicting. The middle classes tend to assume it is all knees up Mother Brown while the working class often imagine it is all middle-class ladies doing pottery. The elderly believe it is for the young; and the young that it is patronised by no one under the age of fifty. Some believe it is too rigid and formal; and others that it is all too improvised and amateur. Some people believe that adult education is to do with training sixteen-year-old Post Office employees; and others that its main function is to provide the disadvantaged with something to keep them occupied. And many without any first-hand knowledge of adult education automatically accuse it of mediocrity.

Some of these misconceptions and prejudices are inherited. Adult education does have a checkered past. It is not so long ago that in some parts of the country adult education centres were segregated into men's and women's institutes and the boot repairing and knees up Mother Brown image may not always have been without basis in fact. And the horror stories handed down about the way absent tutors were replaced by the first person to wander into the office could account for the reputation of mediocrity. But the misconceptions persist and cannot all be put down to history.

Association with School

Using schools in the evening does not always help. It requires faith on entering some adult education premises to believe that anything but a repetition of one's worst school experiences could ever take place in such surroundings. Two women in their late twenties came up the stairs to the top floor at Addison's headquarters one evening, took one look at the timetables on the walls, the people filling in forms, the school cupboards, the classroom doors, the bare floor, the yellow lighting; and turned and fled. I chased after them.

'Can I help you?' I asked, aware that all they wanted to do was get out of the building.

They hesitated. 'I want to improve my spelling', one of them said. 'I can read all right. It's just my spelling.'

'I said I'd come along with her', the other said. They were both hot with humiliation, having half admitted something they may have concealed from others for years — that they had trouble reading and writing.

'You don't have to fill out a form', I said. 'Let me take you to the tutor of the general education class. You can have a talk with her, and see what you think. You don't have to stay.'

As I ushered them into the room I saw it for a moment through their eyes. Small school desks, sticks of chalk, piles of children's workbooks on the day-school teacher's desk, toys, children's pictures on the wall. By bringing these women into the room I was presenting them with a comprehensive array of reminders that as far as reading and writing were concerned they were still infants!

Adult education is the poor cousin, tagging along behind the other sectors, using borrowed premises, understaffed and ill-equipped, so it would be surprising if the image it presented to the world were not a little tarnished — but why had we put the general education class downstairs and not in one of the adult rooms on the top floor?

Nomenclature

Using the nomenclature of the other sectors does not help adult education's image either. The word 'student', for example, is universally used in adult education yet to many has extremely limited connotations, referring exclusively to people in their late adolescence or at the beginning of their adult lives. The use of the word may prejudice some people against adult education, making it difficult for them to distinguish adult education from the very different world of further education and preventing them from fully comprehending that an adult education activity is a co-operative endeavour involving adults of all ages leading full adult lives. By the same token the word 'course' can imply a formality and rigidity of structure that has very little to do with the relaxed atmosphere and flexibility of many adult education activities.

The use of the language of the other sectors can have a subtly corrupting effect on the staff as well. They may be tempted to think only in terms of 'courses' and 'students' and forget the many other complex social and community roles adult education can play. A head of centre bearing the title of 'principal' or 'warden' may find himself adopting autocratic or paternalistic poses and forgetting that his job is to serve fellow adults, not dictate to them. And being the head of a 'college' or 'education institute' he may be tempted to imitate other institutions with the same sort of appellation, providing too many courses at a 'high academic level' rather than a comprehensive range of activities aimed at everyone.[6]

Publicity

But the main explanation for adult education's poor image can usually be found in the poverty and inappropriateness of its own publicity. Adult education tends to publicise itself in the way other educational institutions do—through prospectuses and booklets. These are often dismal affairs, couched in academic and/or bureaucratic language and lacking any attempt at exciting design. Some are little more than time-tables between covers, and others are pompous in tone, opening with an address from 'The Principal' or a quotation from some suitable worthy such as Ruskin or a recent education secretary. Some are difficult to read. And some are mildly insulting. PLEASE ATTEND YOUR CLASSES PUNCTUALLY AND REGULARLY, said one in capital letters, AND REMEMBER TO NOTIFY THE PRINCIPAL OR TUTOR WHEN ABSENCE IS UNAVOIDABLE. (This to adults attending the centre because they want to.)[7]

Relying on the prospectus to publicise adult education is a bad mistake since it presupposes on the part of the prospective student an acquaintance with educational brochures and the patience and ability to work his way through the small print, the cross-references and the timetables. This mistake is further compounded by the fact that the booklets are then left in piles in places such as the local library or sent out to former students and those who ring into the centre with an enquiry, so that only those who already know of the centre's existence or are in the habit of exploring the local services are ever likely to learn what the centre has to offer. It keeps it all in the family. And for those who do not have the first-hand experience of adult education and into whose hands the booklet happens to fall, the tone and style will in all likelihood convey the false impression that adult education is simply more of the same — a part-time repetition of what the other sectors can probably do better anyway.

But adult education is different. Its atmosphere is different, its programme is different, the principles according to which it operates are different, and as a result its publicity should be different. Children are drummed up and marched into school by law. No need for lively, attractive publicity there. And college and university students, although not statutorily required to attend, seek out the institution themselves in order to gain a qualification and get on in the pressing business of earning a living; there is a need for publicity in the form of a comprehensive statement of the options available — information rather than advertisement. But the potential consumers of adult education are adults. They are free agents and under no statutory or professional pressure to attend. As a result, adult education must advertise. It must pull people in by presenting itself as a worthwhile complement or attractive alternative to all the other demands on an adult's free time. In particular it must vie with the welter of other leisure activities society offers — television, cinema, concerts, travel, theatre, the pub — all of which are professionally publicised.

Adult education publicity should perform four functions:

1 Provide information, details, and any advance instructions necessary on individual courses for those who have decided what subject they want to take.

2 Provide information on the full range of options available for those who might want to make use of the adult education facilities but have not yet decided how.
3 Advertise on the open market to let people in the area know what is available and to attract new people in.
4 Combat ignorance and misconceptions by engaging in a programme of public education, telling people what adult education is, how it differs from the other sectors of the education service, and what it can do.

If these are our objectives, then the publicity put out by the travel industry offers an excellent model. For the client who has already decided where to go, the travel industry provides booklets containing detailed information which the client can consult and which the agent can also use for reference. For the client who is contemplating travel but has not yet made up his mind how and where, the travel industry provides a whole range of flip-through brochures covering all the options available and providing enough information to help the client come to a decision. To attract the uncommitted to the idea of travel the industry makes use of a whole range of advertising aids — single-leaf brochures aimed at stimulating interest, leaflet drops, posters and a whole range of advertising in the mass media. And finally the travel industry engages in the whole spectrum of public relations — sponsoring activities, maintaining close links with other industries and institutions, sponsoring articles and supplements on travel in the press, providing ideas for television that will incorporate travel — in order to keep the idea of travel and the awareness of it as a possible option alive in the public mind. Travel publicity is varied, colourful and imaginative and has as its constant theme the idea that travel is an exciting adventure.

Adult education also makes a mistake in the way it times its publicity. Attendance tends to drop off as the year continues. There are several reasons for this: adults move house or change jobs; other demands on their time may increase to a point where they can no longer attend; the course itself may prove too demanding, or may provide what the student wanted much more quickly than anticipated. As a result, by the middle of second term many adult education classes can be down to half-strength. Many of these classes are ongoing activities and can be joined at any point during the year, so that January is clearly the time for a major publicity drive to boost attendance and prevent the closure of classes. Yet most adult education publicity comes in one large dollop in September and is not repeated till the following September. It is certainly not what the travel industry would do.

Lessons Learnt

The survey in the area around the Brackenbury branch made us acutely aware of the shortcomings of Addison's publicity. It had, after all, been difficult asking people what courses they wanted us to provide when they did not know we existed. By sheer good luck the survey coincided with an ILEA decision to decentralise the control of publicity and for the first time Addison was permitted to design its own prospectus and choose what other methods it might use to publicise its activities. The institute radically redesigned its prospectus for September 1974 and in January 1975 organised a 20,000 leaflet drop. In the following January the number was upped to 24,000 and the exercise repeated.

In designing the leaflet the institute tried to take into account the lessons learnt in the survey. The leaflet went out between first and second term and was aimed at supplementing the publicity of the previous September and boosting attendance. It carried information on courses starting that term and comprehensive lists of courses which would welcome new students. It carried a map of the area with the branches marked on it, and the statement from which I have already quoted on page 8. The statement ended with this paragraph:

There are lots of classes and activities you can join when we start up again on 5th January. Have a look through the lists in this leaflet, then come along and try us out. It's amazing what you can learn in just one evening a week.

Addison did not have unlimited funds to spend on the leaflet and it certainly would not have won any prizes for design. There were no illustrations and the colour scheme consisted of black type on yellow paper. But the leaflet had the tone and style of a commercial advertisement and not that of an educational prospectus. It set out to 'sell' adult education. It was a step in the right direction.

Chapter 5

Demand

Participation and Consultation

The aim of the Brackenbury project was to create demand.
The project was planned in four stages — the survey, the public
meeting, the pilot programme, the first full programme — and
the hope had been that a community dynamic would develop
as the project progressed, that people living in the area would
begin taking an active interest in developing the annexe; that
they would talk amongst themselves and begin coming forward
with ideas for courses so that the programme in the annexe
would develop a genuine relevance to them and their area. But
the project never really took off.

There are two reasons for this. The first is the urban
isolation our peculiar century seems to have forced on us. In
the street I surveyed, people of different races, classes and
cultures lived cheek by jowl, yet each apparently moved on his
own plane and virtually ignored his neighbours. There was no
sense of community and it was extremely unlikely that I could
have stimulated any genuine expression of demand simply by
knocking on doors. If I managed to convince one person in
that street that Addison was worth making use of I had
convinced one person only. I had to start all over again next
door.

The second reason is that there was a basic flaw in the
project. Public participation and consultation were newly
popular concepts at the time, particularly in the fields of
public planning, and the Brackenbury project was Addison's
attempt to introduce these practices into the planning of
the Brackenbury annexe. Participation and consultation in

planning decisions are all very well but the public is rarely in the picture right from the start. Usually someone, a professional planner for example, decides that there is going to be a plan and only asks for participation at some later date. This was the case with the Brackenbury project. The institute decided to develop the annexe whether people wanted it or not. All subsequent approaches to the community said in effect: we have decided to develop this annexe along fairly conventional lines but within these limits we are prepared to listen to your suggestions. The institute was definitely not offering the annexe to the community to be used in whatever way they wished, so we were a little naive to hope for a passionate debate to develop and for the demands to come flowing in. In fact throughout the project there was more than a faint echo of the paternalism of the other sectors of the education service, and people must have felt this. *We* had decided to develop the annexe for *them*.

Kenmont

But the spontaneous expression of demand can and does occur. At about the time of the survey I learnt from a community relations officer that the headmistress of Kenmont School had enquired about the possibility of tuition in English for some of her Spanish and Asian parents. Kenmont School was in a district called College Park, a forgotten pocket of houses in the extreme north of the borough. There were about 400 houses in all, mostly two-up and two-down. To the north was a major arterial road and a railway line. To the west another busy road and an industrial estate. To the south several railway lines, a canal, a cemetery, and the vast dreary expanse of Wormwood Scrubs. And to the east another very large cemetery. It was as if a committee of malevolent planners, meeting after midnight, had set out to isolate this collection of houses by every urban and industrial means (save a motorway) at their disposal. English, West Indians, Irish, Indians, Pakistanis, Spanish and an Italian or two lived there. There was a pub, a small general store and some shops and business fronts along the northern periphery of the area, but otherwise the only community facility at the time appeared to be the school. The school worked overtime. It housed a junior and infants school, and a youth club in the evenings, and was the meeting place for boy scouts and girl guides. It was Victorian-style again but had one rounded corner and a half-hearted attempt at a tower, giving it something of the flavour of a castle rising above the streets of largely identical houses clustering around it.

Addison made no provision in the area but I contacted the headmistress and, in the same term as we launched the pilot programme at Brackenbury, Addison set up two English for Immigrants classes on Tuesday evenings in a small annexe in the Kenmont School playground.

The first evening was nerve-racking. The headmistress was there clutching her handbag. The indefatigable school helper, who lived in the area and had backed the idea from the start, was there. The schoolkeeper and his wife were there. And I was there along with the two tutors I had talked into taking on this extra evening's work. As seven o'clock approached and no one had arrived we gave vent to our tension in a quietly agitated debate on the precise time at which we should take a tea-break. At seven o'clock the school helper departed, muttering darkly that she was 'going to get them'.

The first student arrived about five minutes late — a Spanish woman in her thirties, small, immensely friendly, full of laughter at seeing so many people waiting. She sat down with one of the tutors and the rest of us continued waiting. Gradually people arrived. Four more Spanish women and an Italian woman, then an Indian woman. Then three Indian men, a middle-aged Indian woman and her seventeen-year-old daughter were shepherded firmly in by the school helper. Two of the men had come to learn English, and the other had come as a chaperone to his wife and daughter. By half-past seven two classes were under way. There was a lot of laughter from the Spaniards and the Italian and a lot of shyness from the Indians. There were also a lot of people available to make the tea.

Over the next three weeks the classes grew to a stable six or seven students per tutor, and became an established part of the students' week. Two of the Spanish women said that it was their only break from the drudgery of factory and housework, and it seemed likely that the same was true for some at least of the Asian women as well. So far so good. At the request of the headmistress and with the obvious accord of those attending, Addison was providing a useful educational/social/community service.

But the area was small and the community cohesive enough for word to get around about these classes; and the word cannot have been all bad because about half-way through the term the school helper said to me: 'Some of the English and West Indian women are saying that if you're doing English for the Asians and Spanish, why can't you do something like dancing or keep-fit for them?' The institute set up a keep-fit class. Then the schoolkeeper's wife said that some of the women in the area wanted dressmaking. The institute set up a dressmaking class. And within a few months of our hearing of Kenmont we were running a programme of four classes in three subjects every Tuesday evening there.

It may be small beer, but it is significant. People watched as the English classes were set up, talked about it amongst themselves and then asked for keep-fit and dressmaking. There were no surveys, no public meetings, no pilot programmes. There was no social engineering (those Indians the school helper shepherded in on the first evening had been waiting quietly at home for someone to come and fetch them) and no empire-building. All Addison did was respond to demand.

Demand

Adult education is designed in the simplest possible way to respond to demand. It is the other side of the numbers game. If classes can be closed on the basis of attendance, then they can also be set up. That is to say, if you have a group of people eager to pursue some activity or if you have evidence of sufficient community interest you can approach your local adult education agency or centre and ask that a course be arranged, a room and basic facilities provided, and a tutor paid. You are residents of the area and the centre is there for the express purpose of providing for your educational needs. The middle-class woman I interviewed during the survey was right about the Chinese cookery class.

Here is how Addison, having learnt that it must sell itself, expressed its community role in its 1975-6 prospectus:

Adult education is a community service. As well as providing a programme of leisure learning we provide educational support for local community and welfare groups ranging from singing for the Red Cross Over Sixty Club, to English classes in a laundry, to rights courses for a local action group. If you feel there is a way in which we can provide educational support for your community group, please contact us and we will do our best to help you.

While it is careful to define the support it can offer as 'educational' and to leave a loophole in the words 'we will *do our best* to help you', Addison is still making the point that, like all adult education, it is open to direct exploitation by members of the community.

Fourteen, the magic number in ILEA, for example, is not an impossible number of people to gather together if the desire to learn is genuine. A street theatre group could ask for instruction in acting and directing techniques. A neighbourhood council could ask for a course on community newspapers, or the techniques of community self help. A trades council could ask for a course on recent industrial legislation. Of course, it would be misleading to suggest that all adult educators will automatically respond to all requests. Some may resist, preferring a quiet life. Others may simply not have resources readily available. But the logic is there in the system. The guarantee of regular and high attendance works wonders. And the phrase 'community group' is open to very wide interpretation.

Supporting Groups
Adult education has a long tradition of responding to demands of local groups. Most centres will provide facilities for local sports and recreation clubs — London Electricity Board Badminton, the Inland Revenue Football Club, the Hammersmith Morris Men and the like — making full use of the gyms and sports areas of the secondary schools they use in the evenings. And many will provide rooms and tuition for the local bridge

and chess clubs and provide facilities and pay visiting speakers for study groups such as the local history society.

The support has very few strings attached. If a group is conducting an archaeological dig in the area, for example, then the local adult education centre is one of the logical places to hold regular meetings to assess the finds. If members of the group enrol for these meetings and pay the usual fee, then the centre will be able to foot the bill for the tutor and contribute towards the fee for visiting experts. Theoretically the group now comes under the centre's educational control, but the centre is unlikely to presume that it knows better than the group which experts to invite or what form the 'course' should take. In almost every case it will endorse the tutor or speakers the group itself has selected

These activities are unlikely to cause any problems, since they are club extensions of the hobbies and interests normally catered for in a conventional adult education programme. But often an adult education centre has co-operative affiliations with local organisations that do not fit so easily into the conventional or non-controversial pattern. In the area of religious belief, for example, adult education centres will from time to time provide support for organisations that argue from a clearly sectarian point of view. The Central Wandsworth Institute in London runs a course on Buddhism; Stanhope Institute, again in London, sponsors a range of courses on Judaism in conjunction with a local synagogue. The Ealing adult education service has run a course on Catholicism designed and taught by Catholic priests. And Addison has as one of its officially recognised branches the London base of an organisation whose activities are based upon the teachings of the philosopher-mystic, Rudolf Steiner.

Temple Lodge

Temple Lodge is an elegant Regency house set in a small road running south from Hammersmith Broadway to the Thames. It is the London home of the Christian Community, an organisation set up in the 1920s with the help and encourage- ment of Rudolf Steiner and based on his teachings. The Christian Community is 'a modern movement for the rebirth of Christianity'. It is an organisation that has its own priesthood and through its association with the thinking of Steiner a continuing interest in all the fields the Austrian philosopher-mystic concerned himself with—curative education, bio-dynamic farming, eurhythmy, art, homeopathic medicine. In addition to the conducting of services and pastoral work the Christian Community at Temple Lodge publishes its own books and leaflets, holds music concerts and art exhibitions, and runs seminars, conferences and courses on a wide variety of subjects associated with its philosophy and religious beliefs.

The association between Addison and the Christian Community was established when the Community moved into Temple Lodge in the early 1960s. The minister of the Community and the principal of Addison met and as a result a course on psychology was set up at Temple Lodge taught by a member of the Community and supported by Addison. In return the Community provided accommodation for one or two institute courses such as drama and music appreciation. Addison gained use of premises in a corner of its patch where it had formerly been unable to make any provision. In 1970 Addison began using Temple Lodge during the day to run pre-school playgroup leadership courses and, in conjunction with the Christian Community, a course called 'Caring for the Mentally Handicapped Child'. At the same time Addison was beginning to develop its 'special studies' section, supplementing its basic programme of hobbies and interests with a small number of short courses in the humanities and social sciences. It chose Temple Lodge as a suitable place to hold a course on comparative religion, to which it invited as speakers ministers from the various Christian denominations and other religions practised in the area. The minister of the Christian Community suggested other courses to complement the comparative religion course. These were taken on by the institute and in 1971-2 Addison was running or supporting courses at Temple Lodge on four days and four evenings of the week. From the institute's point of view Temple Lodge had become another of its branches and in the 1971-2 prospectus it was listed as such.

These were the courses Addison supported at Temple Lodge on Monday evenings during the 1975-6 year:

'Experiments in Education' — in which teachers working in schools and colleges based on the educational ideas of Rudolf Steiner discussed the methods they used to teach eurhythmy, art, astronomy, natural science and history.

'Whole Foods' — in which farmers, dieticians and doctors discussed organic and bio-dynamic methods of farming and the arguments for various alternative diets.

'Man and Nature' — in which a number of doctors discussed subjects such as sleep, man and the animals, man and the plants, man and the metals, human geography, the nature of poisons, the twelve senses, and evolution from Darwin to Steiner.

All three courses were proposed by the Christian Community and with only one or two exceptions all the speakers were suggested by the Christian Community. Addison administered the courses and paid the speakers. Obviously Addison's staff conferred with the Community and kept a watch on the progress of the courses, but you could argue that all Addison was really doing was paying the Christian Community to put on the Christian Community's courses. It is certainly a neat example of an organisation making very astute use of its local adult education facilities.

Erudite and Inspired People
These things work both ways, however. The courses were open to all comers and were well attended, indicating that Addison was answering a demand. And there was no doubt that those Monday evenings added a rarefied and different flavour to Addison's overall programme. I remember a farmer breaking off during his lecture in the 'Whole Foods' course to talk of the way in which cows, when grazing in a field, placed themselves according to certain forces that centred on and emanated from them. He said their positioning could give a whole meaning to a hillside. He spoke with such conviction and evident joy in what for him was a mystical insight, such a belief in his farm and the rightness of his relationship with nature that it made the methods of intensive and battery farming seem not destructive of the environment nor cruel nor any of the other common criticisms levelled at them, but simply a shallow and selfish experience.

In the 'Man and Nature' course a panel of London homeo-paths took up and examined this question of the rightness or wrongness of our relationship with the world. They argued that scientific man had lost mysticism as a commonplace. One of the doctors saw this loss symbolised in the prevalence of the image of the skeleton figure of death in the sixteenth century. They did not deny the value of scientific progress but saw it as extremely one-sided and argued that a return to a full understanding of the world was to be found in Steiner's style of mysticism. The meanings of 'symbol' and 'reality' were ques-tioned, often reversed, so that in one discussion the brain within the skull was likened in texture and form to the foetus in the womb and a reality seen in this similarity . . . .

The speakers on the 'Man and Nature' course were erudite and inspired people who challenged social and scientific dogma. It was, as all good adult courses should be, a stimulating experience.

Chapter 6

The Adult Course

Women and Men

Adult education activities enjoy extraordinary freedom. Once a group of adults has assembled there are very few external constraints on the direction the activity may take or the character it may assume. Certainly there is no reason why an activity should slavishly imitate the practices of the other sectors of the education service. As long as the group approves, almost anything goes.

In 1973-4 Addison set up a ten-meeting course called 'Women and Men'. It was run by the joint editors of *Spare Rib*, a radical women's magazine, who with the help of guest speakers examined the women's movement, asking the question: 'How will women's liberation change the lives of both men and women?' Sometimes the two women turned up together, sometimes separately, one sitting hunched pensively forward, talking softly, the other brusquely pushing her shock of black curls back from her forehead, smiling suddenly, talking hard. They ran the course as a discussion group, with guests acting more as catalysts than as speakers, starting the discussion perhaps, being closely questioned by the group and tutors, or simply by virtue of their expertise acting as arbiters in a continuing debate. Within an hour of the course starting the layout of the room had been changed, the day-school desks pushed aside and the group arranged in one large circle. The tutors and their guests rarely sat together so that no place in the circle became considered as the point from which statements of unquestioned authority could be made. Sometimes after hearing the guest make an introductory statement, the group would break into two or three smaller groups, coming back into one large group at the end of the evening to share the conclusions reached in the 'buzz groups'.

Thirty students were enrolled, about twenty-five women and five men, ranging in age from the early twenties to late middle age. The group quickly established a freewheeling form of autonomy, treating the two tutors as resources, sources of advice and ideas, but not necessarily the people who took the decisions. One evening, for example, the group decided to invite the husband of one of their members as next week's guest speaker, his qualifications for this role being that he was her husband and could give an account of his reactions to her assertion of her right to be treated as an equal in all respects. He was excellent.

The course went in many directions both because of its form and because so much of the source material was the lives and personalities of the men and women in the group. Speakers included women activists, writers, teachers, a sociologist, that husband, another man actively engaged in the politics of sex role liberation, the founder of a centre for battered wives. There were moments of high feeling. One man walked out. I encountered him ranging angrily about the empty canteen late in the evening.

'It's no good', he said. 'They're talking round in circles. It's becoming just a women's thing. They aren't listening.'

'What are you doing hanging round here?' I asked. 'Why don't you go home?'

'I want to go back in and tell them', he said with a grim look on his face.

There were moments of unforeseen tedium. I walked into the room one evening to find the group listening in antagonistic silence to a man I had not seen before. Apparently he had asked if he could contribute; and the group, having by now wholeheartedly adopted the flexible, unstructured form of the course, had agreed. He had virtually taken over and it was only when the antagonism burst into angry attack that he was silenced and the guest speaker for that evening allowed her say. She spoke, however, into a sullen atmosphere with few willing to discuss. It was an unhappy evening.

But it was the only unsatisfactory evening in the course, and it provided valuable substance for discussion in the weeks that followed. Would the group's reaction, for example, have been so hostile if it had been a woman, not a man, who had so wilfully tried to dominate the evening?

Non-vocational

Most adult education is non-vocational. There are no exams, and adult education centres and agencies rarely offer any kind of certification. A student attends a French class because she has found herself mother-in-law to a Gauloise-smoking Frenchman from Toulon and does not understand him. Another attends because he is taking his holidays in Brittany this year. This is not to deny that people join adult education classes because a knowledge of the subject will help them in their jobs. Another member of that French class may be a businessman who wants to converse more easily with his French counterpart in a Parisian firm. But the motives for attending are real motives, deriving from the students' personal circumstances and interests. No one has come to gain the next rung in the educational ladder, nor for the prestige of having attended, nor for a paper qualification, nor for any of the other irrelevant goals that tend to accompany examinations.

The people attending the 'Women and Men' class came because they cared about the subject; and once the course had proved itself, they cared about the course as well. When an adult educator from another centre came to the third meeting equipped with a tape recorder and asked if he could record part of the meeting for a radio programme on adult education, he was given very short shrift.

'The time's too precious' said one woman.

'I came to attend this course, not make a radio programme' said another.

The directness of these replies was no accident. Because the students had come for genuine reasons, because they cared, the course was free from hypocrisy. No one was trying to prove himself or simulate an interest that was not genuine and as a result the situation quickly developed in which people could be more frank, could more honestly express themselves. The man who walked out did so in real anger. He was not obliged to suppress his anger and stay for fear of missing something essential to his 'success' in the course or an examination at the end of it. And his desire to go back into the room came from an interest in continuing. Nothing else was keeping him there, restlessly pacing the empty canteen.

The man's anger may simply have been hurt pride at the fact that the women were not letting him have his say; but he wanted the group to break into smaller groups in which discussion would be easier. With academic rivalry and ambition removed, people in adult education can enjoy being equals. Social barriers are broken down and they can co-operate in learning. The angry student wanted this experience heightened and finally marched back into the room and told the group so, resulting in the introduction of buzz groups and a further development in the co-operative style of the course.

Syllabus

Without exams there is no need for a rigid, predetermined syllabus. Changes can be made to the course on the spur of the moment. When one of the 'Women and Men' group said her husband would have a useful contribution to make, the group could immediately invite him along. A course can take into account up-to-the-minute developments in the field being discussed. A course on censorship coincided with a much-publicised injunction taken out against a television film on Andy Warhol. Naturally enough, the next two or three meetings were given over to a discussion of the forces at play and to hearing guest speakers on the significance and implications of the injunction procedure. There was no pressure to get on with the scheduled subject for the next meeting.

No rigid syllabus means that a course can start in one direction and end up going in another. A course called 'Man and his Planet' at Addison started as a broad history of the planet but ended up as a very detailed study of present-day environmental problems. In the censorship course the group soon realised that the subject was too limited and the course developed into a discussion, with the help of guest speakers, on the broader issues of freedom and social organisation.

An adult education course does not have to be designed according to the requirements of some national or regional examining board or professional body. It does not have to be a 'standard' course equally meaningful to people in every part of the country. Instead it can take into account local conditions and events. An art appreciation class, in addition to studying the works of the great masters, can also take into account what is happening locally, what is hanging in the local galleries or in the stair-well at the local town hall. Its members can talk to local artists and dealers. A centre's programme of dressmaking classes can take into account the fashions of local ethnic minorities. English classes for immigrants might be tailored to use the language of the local industries in which the majority of the students work.

This lack of rigid definition and syllabus also allows an adult education course to be inter-disciplinary. It can slide across boundaries between subjects, drawing information from a variety of activities. A course on Latin America, for example, might involve dance, music, an evening discussing voodoo, and another on revolutionary priests, politics, sociology, geography, history, and be rounded off with an evening of advice for the traveller from a travel agent and/or a seasoned traveller in that part of the world.

To build this flexibility into the 'Women and Men' course the two tutors acted as co-ordinators rather than tutors in the strictest sense of the word. They ran the course and attended every meeting, but invited guest speakers as the course developed and specific fields of interest were decided on. This avoided a pre-arranged list of titles and lecturers. It recognised that in adult education you have no real idea of what the group of people will be like until they have assembled at the first meeting. And it allowed the two course co-ordinators and the class to discuss the possible speakers and subjects as they went along.

A course run in this way is more likely to be relaxed. The course co-ordinator, knowing the group and the direction the course has been taking, can chip in and prevent his guest speaker from presenting a set piece. This will usually encourage others to question and comment as the speaker goes along, so breaking down the lecture form. And as happened in the

'Women and Men' course, a guest may be invited not to speak but simply to be present as an expert, acting as an arbiter or answering questions. In these circumstances the speaker does not tell the group what he or she thinks they ought to know. They find out what they *want* to know.

Length

Obviously this flexibility can extend to the length of the course as well as its subject-matter. The length of the course can be tailored to suit the subject and the students, and can be open to alteration. Just before Value Added Tax was introduced into Britain, Addision ran a three-meeting course on the tax taught by two sharp-eyed officers from Her Majesty's Customs and Excise. The course proved enough at that length, since all it set out to do was provide an introduction to the tax for the benefit of owners and managers of local shops and small businesses, and information on whom to contact if they had further queries once the tax was introduced. An 'intensive' French course, originally planned as two meetings a week for one term only and making use of a modified teaching style based on an unfashionable amount of rote learning, proved so successful that it was continued through to the end of the year.

In fact the short course is a useful form in which to experiment. It requires only a small commitment on the part of the centre. It is more likely to be attractive both to the person who may be daunted by the prospect of an activity stretching a full year into the future, and to the person who leads too busy a life to contemplate giving over more than a few evenings to an additional activity. And it enables the centre to approach the best people with some hope of roping them in as tutors. A leading film critic, for example, might just be persuaded to traipse out to some unattractive school building on the other side of the city to talk for ten meetings on his abiding passion in the world of cinema, but it is extremely unlikely that he would do it week in, week out, for a number of years. Certainly Addison would never have got the editors of *Spare Rib* to run the 'Women and Men' course if they had not been able to put a limit of ten meetings on their involvement.

Stimulus

Obviously in a ten-meeting course there was no chance of dealing with all the aspects of such a subject, but then this was not the intention. Rather it was to take a short, hard look at some of the issues and send people away thinking. This is probably the most exhilarating freedom adult education enjoys. Since the tutor and the administrator are not charged with the awesome responsibility of getting students through an exam, the course they organise need not be comprehensive. The tutor does not have to cover everything to avoid recriminations at the end of the day. He can dwell on the points he and his class find interesting or feel are truly the most significant. He can seek to stimulate without the obligation to inform fully.

This was the reasoning behind 'Flashpoints of the Twentieth Century'. This was a twelve-meeting course in which the tutor described the crises in certain significant years—1917, 1926, 1933, 1945, 1956, 1968—but avoided any lengthy or detailed background analysis. It was an attempt at a descriptive, non-academic method of presenting modern history—an exercise in 'popular' education. Nor is this tendency to be highly selective limited to the 'liberal studies' subjects. Adult education is a part-time activity and time is precious. In a dressmaking class or a woodwork class both the student and the tutor will be eager to do away with the dross and get on with the information and techniques directly related to making the tunic or the set of fold-in coffee tables or whatever else they have decided together is the aim of the course.

However, adult education should not adopt a cavalier approach to its subject-matter. Its aim is not to provide titillation in the manner of the popular mass media or the entertainments industry, nor would it succeed if it tried to. Even the shortest adult education course involves a commitment on the part of the tutor and students to some sort of extended examination of the subject. 'Flashpoints of the Twentieth Century' may have been 'popular' but it was still a series of penetrating lectures presenting facts that were not always widely known, and was always followed by a discussion in which questions requiring background analysis could be asked. The 'Women and Men' course may have been flexible, informal in atmosphere and discursive, but plenty of hard information was passed on and the course was conducted in a spirit of genuine critical enquiry. After all, the two tutors were leading figures in the women's movement. They were extremely well-informed and their guests were articulate, knowledgeable people involved in the issues being discussed. And since they cared about the subject they were anything but casual or superficial in the way they conducted the meetings.

Edge

To stimulate, a course needs an 'edge', a sharpness of definition which will give the course a character of its own. In 'Flashpoints of the Twentieth Century' the edge was to be found in the title and the fact that the course dealt with the explosive moments of the century. In 'Women and Men' the edge was in the overt commitment of the tutors and the fact that the course made no bones about seeing the question of sex equality in the unsentimental political terms of the women's liberation movement.

Because of the particular freedom adult education enjoys, adult educators can design courses with edge. They can search for new angles to subjects, for ways of making the subject attractive, hard-hitting, stimulating. For some years the adult education service in the borough of Ealing ran a course on psychology, giving it a slightly different slant and a different title each year. In 1976-7 the organiser of adult education and the tutor decided to call it 'Pornography, Obscenity and Psychology'. The title certainly had edge enough to attract publicity in the national press. In the middle of Ealing's enrolment period the *Sunday People* ran a story under the headline: WOW! IT'S DOCTOR LIZ'S PORN CLASS.

PORN is going in the timetable at night-school—complete with full frontal nude pictures and sexy books. While other students slog through their French and history textbooks, the Porn Class of '76 will be poring over girlie magazines like *Playboy* and *Mayfair* .... But it's far from being a nudge nudge, wink wink, after-you-with-the-sexy-textbooks night away from the wife. For a start the course lecturer is a GRANNY ....

The course description that appeared in the Ealing booklet *Active Leisure* was couched in slightly more staid language:

> It is the intention of this course to elucidate through psychological analysis the recurring social concern with pornography and obscenity. To do this seriously and objectively it will be first necessary to present some of today's reputable psychological theories, especially those that attempt explanations of unconscious sexual motivation and those that offer analysis of how sexual contacts and social media of communication influence human sexual behaviour . . . .

As well as being a grandmother, the tutor was an experienced adult education tutor and a respected psychologist and criminologist. What she and the organiser were trying to do was give a serious course in social psychology an edge by relating it to a matter that gives rise from time to time to excited public debate. This they succeeded in doing to an almost ludicrous extent, since the course was advertised amidst a national furore over a Danish film-maker's announcement that he intended coming to England to make a film on the sex life of Jesus Christ.

Courses with an edge like 'Women and Men', 'Flashpoints of the Twentieth Century' and Ealing's excursion into the exciting world of pornography are departures from the standard course. They are not aimed at the student who wants a course in a particular subject and is looking for the one nearest home. Rather they are designed to pull in people who, until they saw the course advertised, were not contemplating attending a course at all. In 1974 in an attempt to break free from the standard cinema appreciation course based on Eisenstein *et al.*, Addison set up a course on horror and monster movies. The tutor was a professional film critic fascinated by these two genres who had an encyclopaedic knowledge of the film industry, and the ability to ask uncomfortable questions. The course pulled in about twenty people who became engrossed in the subject.

'Imagine me in an evening class' said one of them during coffee-break about half-way through the course. But he was.

And he was back in another, this time on commercial cinema, the following year.

Earlier I said that adult education can stimulate without the obligation to inform fully. Another way of expressing this is to say that adult education is as much about discovery as it is about study. But the hope is that once people have been stimulated, once they have discovered a new interest, then, like the cinema student, they will go on. The hope is that they will attend other courses, make more demands on their centre, make use of other community facilities—libraries, lectures, other educational institutions, the media, individual contacts —in order to follow up their interest.

Co-operative Activity

Some members of the 'Women and Men' group did continue. About fifteen of the women formed a group that continued meeting regularly in members' flats and houses. Three years later this group approached Addision and asked that another course be set up. The institute agreed, and appointed three of the group as course tutors. This is the description they wrote:

'A WOMAN'S PLACE?'
This course is designed to stimulate broadbased discussion on the changing roles and relationships between men and women in our society. The discussion will be led by course tutors and visiting lecturers and will be flexible and allow for maximum participation by members of the group.

The tutors, having been through the mill themselves, recognised that adult education is a co-operative activity and formulated a statement saying as much. This simplest and most important feature of adult education underlies everything in this chapter. For an adult education course is essentially a group of adults pooling their knowledge and skills, with the tutor acting as encourager, arbiter, adviser, questioner and group-member as well as teacher. An adult education course is an exercise in sharing.

PART II
People

Chapter 7

Tutors and Students

Equals

Adult education is an activity among equals. Tutors are not in a position of unquestioned authority. Perhaps they can claim superiority in their knowledge of the specific subject but they can make no such assumption in any other field of human activity. The tutor of an English for Immigrants class learnt this when he strayed from the business of teaching basic English for long enough to misquote Shakespeare and was promptly corrected by one of his students who may have been little more than a beginner in colloquial twentieth-century English but had at one stage been a lecturer with a specialist interest in Shakespeare's England at a university in eastern Europe. A speaker invited to address a course on the youth movement of the 1960s made an ill-considered reference to Marx and was shot down by a woman of seventy-four who prefaced her remarks with the words: 'Speaking as a lifetime member of the Communist Party. . . .'

The situation can even arise when a tutor is no longer sure of his advantage in the subject he is ostensibly there to teach. For two consecutive years Addison ran a ten-meeting course in the subject area of criminology. The tutor was a research criminologist, highly qualified and in touch with the latest information. She could have been forgiven for assuming that in a 'popular' criminology course at a common or garden adult education centre she would know a great deal more about her subject than anyone in the class. But among her 'students' over the two years, as well as those there out of general interest, were a chaplain from one of the country's largest prisons, a prison education officer, a prison training officer, several people from the social services, a leading figure from Radical Alternatives to Prison, and a young man from the Elephant and Castle who announced that he was a professional criminal and had come to learn what the other side was saying about him. The tutor found herself an expert among experts. She had intended to give a series of lectures but as the course got under way naturally modified her approach, adopting a much more democratic and flexible form.[8]

A Punch-up

Running a course in a flexible and democratic way can have its dangers. In a course called 'Television', which was advertised as 'a mixture of theory and practice using the basic equipment of camera, recorder and monitor', the tutor began conventionally enough, examining with the help of guest experts the way in which the BBC and ITV were organised, the way in which the number of channels were parcelled out, and the possible alternatives such as cable television and local television stations. Tapes of BBC and ITV programmes were shown and discussed, and then compared with video tapes made by several community groups. At the fourth meeting the tutor began moving from theory to practice, letting the group handle the video kit for the first time and instructing them in its use. From that evening on he adopted the practice of having members of the group operate the kit at all times, recording group discussions or whatever else was going on in the room, so that everyone could have as much experience as possible in the simple mechanics of recording vision and sound. It was at this fourth meeting also that the tutor shifted the control of the course to the group by beginning discussions on various practical projects they might engage in, and asking them to decide.

From that meeting on, one of the group began playing a prominent part in the group discussions, often disagreeing with the tutor's suggestions. A personality clash developed and during the seventh meeting the tutor hit him. This alone is remarkable enough, but what is much more remarkable is the fact that by the seventh meeting the group were sufficiently adept at operating the video kit to be able to record in vision and sound the build-up to the incident, the incident itself, and the extraordinary wind-down after the blow had been struck. It made twelve minutes of riveting television.

The tape cut in on a conversation. The group were sitting in the canteen after coffee-break. Two discussions were taking place, one centred on the student who was talking about what he and several others had been doing with the video kit in the canteen while the other classes were taking their break. The tutor had stopped them and the student was angry.

The camera shifted to the other group, who were discussing a project for the following week with the tutor. The camera zoomed in and the tutor, studied in close-up, looked as if he had had one of those days. The two conversations drew together and became a tense discussion between the tutor and the student. The tutor argued that the sub-group in the canteen had not been doing what the class had decided. The student maintained that what they had been doing was an *extension* of what the class had decided.

'*We* thought it was a good idea' said a woman.

'Don't get so excited' someone else said.

'I'm not getting excited,' the student said, 'but I don't like the way he ripped me off in public.'

The tutor stood up. At this point the action outstripped the camera operator but not the sound operator. Shot of the tutor's thigh.

'I did not rip you off in public!' shouts the tutor.

Shot of a sudden movement. The woman's shoulder jerking out of the way. The tutor's waist line lunging forward. Resounding smack.

'Get out of my class!' shouts the tutor, followed by a stunned silence in which the camera catches up with events and from then on follows with inspired skill. The tutor, the student and the woman are all on their feet. They are staring at each other. There is a zoom-in to the student and the woman, then a whip-pan to the tutor, white with fury, choking over his words, fighting for logic in his phraseology. The exchange is rapid, low and tense, and surprisingly they are still talking about the various class projects. Here the camera pans quickly across the rest of the group, all still sitting. There is a zoom-in on one young woman staring at the floor, a glance at a man in the group, then up and back to the protagonists.

'It's just that I won't have you trying to take over my class,' the tutor is saying, 'so I think you had better leave.'

The tutor walks away and sits down. The camera pans with him, then sweeps back to the student and the woman. Their faces are grim, drawn. The sound is not with them and you can see their lips moving in tense, quiet conversation, but can only hear background noises. They decide to leave, and walk into and across camera, blotting out the image for a moment. The image clears and is in close-up of the tutor, who is sitting looking at the floor with the remainder of the class in a rough circle around him. There is a long moment's silence in which the camera watches the tutor's thoughts. It is a remarkable piece of tape. You can see the tautness in the tutor's jaw, his eye, his mouth, the fight for control, then the tortured look up.

'I'm sorry about that' he says quietly.

'If we could interview a local politician . . . ' says one of the group immediately and they are back discussing the project for next week.

The tape ran on for another two minutes or so. All the edgy immediacy of *cinéma vérité* was gone. The camera work was unhurried. The tape showed an interesting-looking group of adults discussing an interesting-sounding video project and occasionally seeking expert advice from their pensive but reasonably attentive tutor.

The matter could not rest there. The incident had been witnessed, open-mouthed, by one or two students from other classes who were still in the canteen. And understandably, the student who had been struck complained. The centre had to act officially, but it was all done in a thoroughly adult fashion. The tutor and his student met, and apologies were given and accepted. The two men even played the tape through. And at the following meeting the tutor and the student walked into the room together and the group began work on the project they had been discussing at the end of the tape.

The group continued meeting for the rest of the scheduled

twelve meetings and then elected to go on for another term in order to make a tape on a theme in keeping with International Women's Year. They shot and edited a tape entitled 'Women Talking' which they entered into a national video exhibition. The tape was well received and for about a year was in some demand by women's groups. The group who had stayed on then formed the nucleus of a tutorless 'course' in the centre's programme for the following year under the title 'Video Project'. Despite the brief eruption into violence in that first term, the tutor's decision to follow a democratic form had paid off.

Chapter 8

Tutors

The *Russell Report* estimated that the number of part-time tutors in adult education in all its forms in England and Wales 'probably approaches 100,000' (para. 395).[9] Here are four of them:

The Professional

The television tutor was a tall, articulate man. From university he went into television, spending five years mainly in current affairs and documentaries. He then left and worked as a television critic, journalist and free-lance writer, developing an interest in community video and community access to television. At the time of the course he was working in radio. He was not a trained teacher. He was a professional communicator who was prepared to give one evening a week to share his ideas and professional expertise with others.

Adult education can make excellent use of professionals like the television tutor. A woodwork tutor need not be a trained teacher from a college or school but can be a local carpenter and builder during the day who gives his one adult class per week the tips that only a practising professional will know. The pottery tutor can be a professional potter whose teaching will take into account the pressures of the market-place and whose aesthetic sense will be under constant review in discussion with other professional potters. The dressmaking tutor can be a cutter in a fashion house, the folk guitar tutor the owner of a local musical instrument shop, or a performing artist who plays the club circuit, or a busker for that matter.[10]

Why should these professionals spend their evenings muddling around with a bunch of amateurs? You will get all sorts of answers to this question, but many true professionals are humble about their skills and again and again you will hear this remark: 'I learn as much as they do'.

The Horse's Mouth

It is common policy at Addison to employ language tutors who speak the language as their mother tongue. One French tutor was a slender, dark-haired woman born and brought up in Paris but of Corsican background and looks. She had visited England several times to study English, and at the age of twenty-four married a language teacher and settled in London. She completed her English studies and after the birth of her first child began looking for part-time work. She approached Addison Institute and was offered a French beginners' class on Friday evenings. She had never taught before and her only qualification for the job was that she was French herself. She attended two 'in-service training' meetings for new tutors in the fortnight before she started and then was thrown in the deep end, basing her first encounter with the class on a book recommended by another tutor and some general teaching hints from her husband.

She struggled through the first year learning the hard way — and teaching a beginners' language class on Friday evenings during the winter months certainly is the hard way. But she and her class survived and in the following year she was given two classes a week. Now she began to look beyond simple survival for ways of improving her teaching. She began using film strips, records and tapes, and began building up a collection of her own slides, cartoons, articles, and other teaching aids. By 1977-8 she was teaching four classes a week — as many as she could handle in addition to her family and other commitments — and was considered one of the best of the institute's language teaching staff. In all that time she received no formal training. She had attended meetings and conferences of language tutors from time to time, but for the most part, like a large number of adult education tutors, her skill had been developed in the classroom by trial and bitter error.

There is a simple logic in using the French tutor described above rather than, say, an English man or woman with a degree in modern languages and formal teaching qualifications. Her students were not learning a language as an exercise. They were learning French in order to get by in France and the French tutor, being French, could provide them not only with 'Academy French' but with slang and Parisian argot as well. She could invite along French friends from time to time to meet the group, or her sixteen-year-old nephew when he was passing through London to give an advanced class a taste of the way the teenagers were talking. And she could provide her classes with information that would help them gain entry to various aspects of French life when they next visited the country—contacts, places to visit, restaurants recommended by her friends, films the French were currently raving about, trend-setting exhibitions, and so on.

As students will testify, there is something special about getting the story from the horse's mouth. 'I mean,' said one of her students at the end-of-year party, 'the way she dresses, the way she looks, the way she talks, everything about her is so *French*.'

The language tutor is an unsensational example of the way in which adult education can employ as tutors people who have lived the experience rather than those who have made an academic study of it. Adult education can present the living case history. The tutor for a course on China can be someone who has lived there. For a course on comparative education speakers can be people who have taught in the countries being discussed, or parents who have put their children through school there, or the children themselves. And for a course on comparative religion, speakers can be the exponents and adherents of the faiths being considered. Rather than listen to an English academic on the Sikh religion, an adult education group can listen to a Sikh, perhaps visit his temple. In this way adult education can be a warmer, more human experience, less artificially cut off from the matters being discussed.

The Passionate Amateur

One of the most successful classes Addison runs is called 'Know Your London' and is a survey of London's art, architecture and sculpture. Year after year the course is packed out — fifty entranced adults crammed into a school classroom designed to hold not more than thirty school-children. They include local people there out of general interest, people visiting London for a year or two, trainee guides who have heard about the course, and even the odd professional guide keeping himself up to the mark. The tutor is by general agreement brilliant. His knowledge is encyclopaedic, his presentation skilful and endlessly amusing, and the amount of work he puts in to prepare the courses enormous. He has the kind of devotion to the subject and wealth of knowledge you would expect to find in an art historian of high calibre, or just conceivably an architect or professional guide — someone whose full-time professional occupation dealt with or overlapped to a considerable extent the subject of his course. But this is not the case. During office hours the tutor is a tax inspector.

The tutor is in his early fifties, a big energetic man with thinning, sandy-red hair. He is a Staffordshire man and started his working life as a colliery geologist when he was drafted into the mines after the war, making use of his school and one year's technical college training in geology. From that post he progressed to colliery surveyor, gaining surveying qualifications and developing an interest in architecture as he went. While working as a colliery surveyor he looked into the law relating to the mining industry and when he left the mines and joined the Inland Revenue he took a law degree. He was now working in London and as a leisure pursuit he began to explore London, following up his interest in architecture and researching the city's history. His decision to teach a course on London came when he enrolled as a member of a group that made regular study tours of London. 'The chappie taking the group knew his way round the streets of London better than I did but I found I knew more about the art and architecture than he did.' With the same application that had gained him his qualifications in geology, surveying and law, he now attended courses to qualify himself as a London guide and began amassing slides and documents and teaching aids. He then applied to Central London Adult Education Institute and ran the first of his courses.

In the classroom he talks hard and fast, and fires questions at his class relentlessly in a mock imitation of the army instructor. The only difference is that the answer is always obvious or actually on the board or screen in front of the students' eyes when he asks the question. It is a trick that produces a lot of laughter but has the same effect as a question genuinely testing your knowledge. You go away remembering. He says he learnt to teach when training to be a scoutmaster.

Having become such an expert in the field, has he ever thought of teaching full-time or taking a job in the art world? 'No.'

Why does he teach?

'I enjoy it.'

Many adult education tutors are passionate amateurs, people who have a consuming interest which they must communicate to others. Adult education provides them with an outlet for this communication and gains totally committed tutors into the bargain. Cinema tutors often come into this category. A tutor of a course on science fiction in all likelihood will. Some language tutors and almost all yoga tutors will.

Some of them have to be watched. One yoga tutor taught for a whole year without bothering to claim payment for her services. Finally the full-time staff had to fill out all her pay claims and virtually force her to sign them. And not all passionate amateurs automatically make good tutors. Some breathlessly attempt to communicate everything in the first half-hour and exhaust themselves and their students in the process. Others preach. But their interest gives them drive and if this is accompanied by any sort of teaching skill they can, like the 'Know Your London' tutor, become second to none.

The Teacher

Adult education also makes use of professional teachers. Many do it for extra pocket money but some do it because they enjoy the liberating atmosphere of adult education. Freed from the fetters of an examination syllabus and working with a group of non-captive adults they can tackle their subject anew, vary their approach to it. The dressmaking tutor from a college of fashion might take on an evening at the local adult centre to run a course called 'Clothes in a Hurry' in which she teaches busy adults the short cut for rapid effect rather than the detailed technique she must drum into her daytime students. The domestic science teacher who has to teach a standard cookery course to school-children might stay on after school one evening a week and teach a group of adults *provençale* dishes just to keep her hand in.

In 1974 - 5 Addison decided to try out a twelve-meeting course in second term aimed at students in the institute's various language classes who might be interested in looking at how languages worked, how they could be described and how they differed from one another. The course was called 'Language' and was in effect a short introduction to linguistics. To find a tutor for the course I approached the department of linguistics at one of London's university colleges. One of their lecturers promptly agreed.

He was twenty-nine years old, married, had a baby son, and lived in an outer borough. He dressed in dark or neutral colours, and spoke in a dry careful manner, pausing to ponder from time to time before going on. He could be very ironic, and from the moment you met him you were sure he was no one's fool. He taught the course in an almost rigorously conventional way—chalk and talk followed by questions and discussion. The students sat in serried ranks. Questions were answered in a serious, studied way, the rest of the group forgotten and all his attention directed at the questioner for as long as was necessary to answer in full. Discussion was always directed through him as the lecturer.

A mixed group of people—some who had joined a beginners' class the previous term in one of the eight languages the institute offered, some who had been attending classes for several years, an Iranian who spoke several languages fluently—attended week after week as the lecturer delved deeper and deeper into the methods of describing and differentiating languages, filling the blackboards slowly and deliberately at each meeting with the symbols and codes of his subject. Step by ordered step he initiated the group into the discipline of linguistics, leaving no one behind and earning the group's unanimous praise.

Some time after the course I had lunch with the lecturer at his college. I asked him why he had taken the course in the first place.

'I would not be completely honest if I did not tell you that I had just bought a house and had mortgage commitments to meet', he said. 'Every little bit of extra cash helped.'

'Would you have taken the course anyway?'

Pause to consider. 'Yes I probably would. People don't know immediately what linguistics is. If I met someone on a bus and he asked me what I did and I said I taught linguistics he probably wouldn't be any the wiser. I'd still be explaining fifteen minutes later. The course was a challenge to explain to a group of people what linguistics was.'

'Did you enjoy the class?'

'Yes, I got very involved. I'd get home with the adrenalin still pumping through my veins. Often I couldn't get to sleep till one or two in the morning. And I like teaching adults. I went to university as a mature student myself.'

'What did you do before?'

The lecturer looked at me for a moment.

I went to a minor public school and it was assumed I was clever and would go on to Cambridge, until I did very badly in my 'O' levels. Then they tried to put me in a lower stream where you did metalwork and learnt to add money, so I left. I worked in a bookshop for a while and then a friend got me a job playing bass in a rock group. The group went to Germany as a resident group in a club in Stuttgart. I moved from bass to keyboard and a group of us formed our own band. We were one of the first soul-rock groups. The singer was a black American who had come over with the US airforce. I played organ and spent five years on the road lugging it about. It was very heavy. We played in Germany and England. We played at one of the big shows at Wembley, had a record in the charts. We were quite big. Then the group split up and if I had wanted to go on I would have had to start right back at the beginning, forming another group and working my way up in the clubs and on the road all over again. I didn't want to do that so I studied for some 'A' levels on my own money and then when

I was looking through university prospectuses I saw a course in linguistics at York and I applied. I gave the Greek master at my school as my academic reference. I don't think any of the other masters would have remembered me. York rang him up and asked him whether he really meant what he had said and he told them that they should take a risk with me. They did, and I found it was exactly what I wanted to do. When I'd finished the degree course they asked me to stay on and teach and then I got the job here. I sometimes miss the rock scene but this is what I really want to do. I sold off the organ and all the other instruments one by one. I don't even have a guitar in the house now.

Chapter 9

A Cruel Test

Sink or Swim

Adult education is a cruel test of a tutor's skill. It is a sink or swim business. If the tutor does not have what it takes, people stop coming. His students vote with their feet, unobtrusively transferring to other classes or simply staying away. It is an unpleasant experience for the tutor. The class dwindles week by week, leaving him all too aware that he has been found wanting, until the centre finally puts him out of his misery by closing the class down. A professional teacher from another sector of the education service who has taught captive pupils for years to his own and his superiors' complete satisfaction may find his one brief attempt to teach an adult education class a horrible moment of truth.

The French tutor was thrown in the deep end and because she was a naturally gifted tutor she (and her class) survived. It all smacks a little of the tough world of American journalism as portrayed by Hollywood in which the young reporter is sent to cover a story on his first day at work and if he can he does and if he cannot he does not come back. Obviously adult education centres do try to provide support in the form of induction courses, in-service training and advice but the poor cousin normally does not have enough full-time staff to guide new tutors carefully through their first meetings. In the vast majority of cases they are given a few general hints, patted on the back and then shoved in front of the class. Some sink.

Survival Pack

Obviously adult education tutors, in common with teachers, instructors and trainers in any field, must know their subject and be able to communicate it. But there are a number of skills and qualities that become particularly important in the adult education context.

In order to survive in adult education, tutors must be able to deliver the goods in neat, clearly identifiable packages. Adult students want results in exchange for the sacrifice of their time, so that a course must be seen, step by obvious step, to be leading somewhere—to a keener appreciation of the plays they see, to a fuller understanding of their children's pre-school development, to a knowledge of yoga, to a better ability to express themselves. Students must never feel that they are wasting their time. Nor can tutors prove themselves at the outset and then slack off for a bit. They must *continue* delivering the goods. Adult students make the decision to attend week by week and will only come if they can say to themselves: 'It was worth it last time'.

Because tutors are in direct competition with the entertainments industry, what they provide must be enjoyable. There is nothing extraordinary about this. Good teaching is usually enjoyable, entertaining even, but in adult education this aspect is vital. Adult students must never be bored, and after a full day's work their boredom threshold may be low.

Adult education tutors must be good with people. They must be capable of moulding disparate collections of adults into working groups and of creating a relaxed and friendly atmosphere. It is an education all by itself to watch the 'Know Your London' tutor welcome a new student into the group. The class comes to an immediate halt as the student comes through the door. The tutor is effusive in his welcome, often making a quick joke and always eliciting the student's name and something else about him while he is still standing. The tutor then quickly directs the new student to a place, often fetching and placing the chair himself, and takes up where he left off. It is very deftly done. The new student is made to feel wanted, introduced and given an identity within the context of the group, then quickly removed from the spotlight and allowed inconspicuously to settle into his new environment alongside someone who will look after him if maps or documents have to be shared. Or watch the French tutor put her beginners at ease at their first meeting. Within a few minutes she has them arranged in threes, exchanging two phrases in French. There is always a lot of laughter and a sense of pleasure at the quick departure from the formal classroom arrangement. It also means that the students go to their first coffee-break having met two people, having overcome with those other two their embarrassment at their ignorance of the French language, and having actually conversed in French.

And adult education tutors have to care. Adult students will not tolerate a nonchalant approach. They must be able to discern a genuine concern for the subject in everything the tutor says and does. If they do, then their tolerance of a tutor's shortcomings will be high. When the television tutor lost his temper and took a swing at one of his students he did so because, rightly or wrongly, he believed the student was disrupting the class. For the others there the whole incident must have been excruciatingly embarrassing, but it was obvious that the tutor cared and they came back in full force the next week. And the full-time staff of the centre were made to realise that the tutor cared, too. At the end of that eventful evening when the group had dispersed and the staff member responsible for audio-visual aids went into the room to lock up the video kit she found the video tape placed carefully to one side with a note in the tutor's handwriting attached to it, saying: 'Do not wipe this tape'.

I asked the tutor why he had made sure such damaging evidence against him was not destroyed.

'I thought it might make an interesting piece of video' he said.

Chapter 10

Students

The Russell Report put the number of students 'aged eighteen and over enrolled on non-vocational adult education courses' at close on two million.[11] Here are four of them:

The Literacy Student
When this 62-year-old woman was asked to talk about herself and her class, this is what she said:

> I have lived in England for more than twenty years now but I come from Jamaica. When I went to school my sister took to education but I didn't. I could write my name and I could read anything easy but nothing hard. They sent me to sewing school, and when I came over here I worked in a factory as a machinist. I sent for my two children and after a while I bought this house. Now my children are both married and I have ten grandchildren. I see some of them every day and at church on Sunday. I am retired now but I still do some work at home. I make anything—hats, dresses, blouses, skirts, nightdresses, clothes for the children. When I came over here I didn't bother much with my reading. With my work and the children I didn't have the time. Two years ago, I went to my doctor and when he gave me a prescription I asked him to show me where I had to mark that I was sixty. He asked me if I wanted to go to reading classes and rang up the school and arranged an interview for me. Now I go to class two evenings a week, and I really enjoy it. We are all different ages, although I'm not the only retired person. Nobody's embarrassed. We don't fret. If you

don't know, you just ask the teacher. She's very nice. Very
relaxed. I used to get my children to write my letters, but
now I can write them myself. I'm not giving up my classes.
I think the only thing I've envied anybody is a good
education.

The Community Activist

There is a community action group in Hammersmith one of
whose functions is to man a welfare rights stall in Shepherd's
Bush market on Saturdays, giving out leaflets and answering
questions on housing, unemployment benefit, supplementary
benefits and civil rights. A leading member of the group is a
quietly spoken man in his early thirties who works as a
production development engineer for a large corporation. He
was brought up in a village in Yorkshire, then another in
Lancashire, then moved to London where he finished his
schooling and went on to university.

I got involved in the welfare rights movement through
Addison Institute. I was twenty-five and living in a bed-
sitter. I looked round for something to do and decided to
join an evening class. I thought of doing a cinema course
but decided to join a course called 'Alternative Societies'
instead. Near the end of the course a member of staff
came in and asked whether anyone was interested in helping the local community relations council run a rights
stall during the summer. I volunteered and once I got
involved I looked round for courses on rights issues. I
went to several more at Addison over the next three years —
one on civil liberties, one on race relations, another on
planning. When the group had got enough volunteers
together for the stall we asked Addision to help train
them. The institute runs a welfare rights course for us every
year now.

The Perennial

'I've never really ceased studying' says one of Addison's most
regular students. She is seventy-eight, tiny, wearing spectacles,
slacks, and a sleeveless cardigan. She speaks with a classless
accent, often leaning forward, her knees pressed together,

making every sentence count, rather as if she were forever disputing a point at a meeting. She was one of six children in a civil servant's family. She left school at fourteen, going out to work as a typist and secretary. In 1925 she joined the London Socialist Choir where she met a family who were members of the Communist Party of Great Britain, and in 1926 she joined the party as well.

It was through the party that she met her husband. He was an engineer and when he went to Russia in 1933 to work for the second five-year plan she followed him. She found the experience 'hard but extraordinarily worthwhile.' Her husband worked in a tractor factory, then a factory that built sections for bridges, while she took different kinds of work to make ends meet. It was the time of the purges; and at three o'clock one morning the police came and took away the husband of a couple with whom they were sharing a flat. In 1938, with the war on the horizon, she and her husband, along with most other foreigners, were asked to leave.

In 1954 after an accumulation of years of disquiet she tore up her party card, but ten years later, at her husband's funeral, she approached the party secretary and asked if she could join again. 'I shall never leave the party again,' she says, 'but I won't be kept in a straitjacket. I'm not going to sacrifice all my time to politics. I want to extend my interests into the wider cultural field in order not to become bigoted.'

At seventy-eight she has two jobs, an hour's typing most mornings for a prominent member of London's Asian community, and then a full day's work in a small agency which deals in real estate and runs minicabs. She remains an active honorary member of a clerical trade union and a member of the cooperative movement. She still travels and has been to France, Germany, Hungary, Bulgaria, Ireland, Albania and America.

In the evening she goes to meetings and adult education classes. 'This year I'm doing anthropology and badminton.'

Badminton?

Let me tell you about my badminton class. I joined last year.

They tried to tell me there would be too much running about but I told them pensioners were allowed to join any of their classes. But the tutor wouldn't let me play on the court like the others. I couldn't hit the shuttlecock and he made me practise out in the corridor, so this year I looked for another tutor at another branch. I told him I was determined to learn and he was very nice. I've played table tennis before but badminton is different. I couldn't serve and I couldn't hit one back. On the third meeting I still hadn't hit a serve and when we went for a break I told the tutor I must have some sort of mental block. Then all of a sudden when we went back from break I tried holding the shuttlecock differently.

Here she jumps up to demonstrate excitedly.

You see, he had told me to hold my arm out like this but then I couldn't reach it with my racket. I held it closer in like this and I got three serves over the net. He was very pleased with me. I thought, well what's happened here? What did I do during break? I must have had a pint of beer or a glass of vodka or something!

Over the years she has attended adult education classes in philosophy, book-keeping, table tennis, German, French, yoga, writing, dancing, and any number of socio-political subjects. 'Oh, and Esperanto, I had a go at that.' Whenever she has been able to she has gone to the Communist Party summer school. And she has studied Russian, attending classes on and off since 1925. 'I've been doing Russian at Addison for the last five or six years but I'm not going this year. I'm keeping an evening free because I have applied to a local theatre group for an audition. There's no reason why they shouldn't take me if I prove I can learn the lines.'

The Writer
Some years ago I was the tutor of a creative writing class in a London centre. The group fairly quickly settled down to about fifteen regulars. One of these was a man in his late twenties, who would sit apart from the others in the class, his fists

clenched and his face taut. He rarely commented on the work read by the others, and sometimes when I questioned him directly he would simply stare unblinkingly, communicating anger and tension. He would wait for his turn, and then he would read.

A lot of what the others read was at one careful remove from their real lives. A civil servant wrote westerns, an American woman wrote stories about an Italian village, a retired nurse wrote stories about children's wards. A young public relations consultant wrote anecdotes concerning his flatmates ('The Spaghetti Incident'). But the man was different. This is the first paragraph of one of the first stories he read in class:

> I have suffered for some time from what the great men call a psychosomatic illness. I know it is physical, but however that is another story. Anyway, to gain relief from my illness I started taking heroin, morphine and methadrine. I had been using heavy for about two years.

His voice was low and dark. Some of his syntax was bizarre and he misused certain words, but these minor peculiarities did not detract from the power of the subject-matter or the driving rhythm of his prose. He would finish reading and I would call for discussion. He would swivel his head and look at whoever was commenting but you could see he was not really listening. The story had been written and read. It was over.

Just once he read out a story using a central character with a name:

> Joe was just starting his fifth sentence for petty theft. Joe felt very bitter about this. He thought, fancy giving me half-a-stretch for nicking a lousy pullover . . . .

The figure was a recidivist who at the end of the story walks out of gaol, has one cup of tea and, in order to raise money for the big job he has told his fellow inmates he intends pulling, steals a camera from a nearby supermarket and is immediately arrested. The last paragraph of the story begins:

> Fancy giving me half-a-stretch for nicking a lousy camera . . . .

The class laughed out loud at the end of the story, but instead of looking gratified the man stared round at the rest of the group, his face dark and troubled. One evening he read a story about a crazed walk through the night streets of London. The story started at 'The Dilly', ranged through Soho, along Oxford Street, through Camden, Kilburn, Hampstead and ended in a cemetery just before dawn with the first-person figure clawing at the earth, mad with grief at his own condition, shrieking and wailing like an animal. No one laughed at the end of this one.

At the beginning of the year the pieces he wrote were short, but as the year continued they became longer and, now that he had us in his mesmeric grip, more self-indulgent. I tried suggesting he edit certain passages but he never re-worked anything.

When the year came to an end and the group disbanded he began ringing me up and calling round to my flat, bringing stories to read. He would arrive early on Saturday morning and stay till late at night, then appear at our door again early on Sunday morning. He dominated the summer. Sometimes he would sit, his muscles so taut that he was in actual pain. He would rail against the doctors who told him his illness was not 'physical'. 'I can *feel* the pain' he would say.

During this summer he began writing a book. He rang me up late one night. 'I've done thirty thousand words already' he said. 'I'm putting it all down.' He came round the following weekend and read for hours. It started when he was seventeen. It recorded trivia, pointless incidents, endless cups of tea in grimy cafés. There were passages of real power but they were lost in a torrent of words. He flicked through, choosing particular incidents, and I seized on this, pointing out that he was reading an edited version so why did he not edit as he wrote, or at least go back and cut out all those cups of tea. He looked angrily at me. 'I'm writing the truth' he said. 'This is what really happened.'

The next year started and he was back in my class, but the split over the question of editing widened. He dominated the group again and we started going round in circles. I would argue that he must edit and he would insist that what he was putting down was 'the truth'. I grew increasingly angry.

Resentment in the group began building up against him and one woman in particular, a fashion model, black-haired and beautiful, began criticising him.

I did not witness the crunch. At the end of the term a married couple invited the group back to their flat for a Christmas drink. I could not go, but I understand that the model mocked him and that the others laughed. He did not come back to the class after Christmas.

Some weeks into the New Year the public relations consultant rang me. He had encountered the man in the street. 'He looked strange,' he said. 'Perhaps we should try and find him.'

I got his address from the class register and we drove there the next evening. He was living in a room over a shopfront in a suburban back street. He let us in but then went on to the attack. The public relations consultant slumped down into a chair but the man and I remained standing, confronting each other while he ruthlessly listed my faults. Much of what he said hit home. Towards the end he said that he would come back to the class. But when we left, the public relations consultant shook his head and said: 'He won't'. And he was right. Whatever that gifted and disturbing writer was going to do next, he did not want us.

Chapter 11

The Adult Educator

Full-time heads of adult education centres or tutor-organisers for the WEA or staff lecturers in university extramural departments[12] are usually short of staff and unable to delegate responsibilities satisfactorily. As a result they have to be many things:

Entrepreneur
They have to be entrepreneurs. They are setters-up of courses, designers of educational programmes, and to do this they must have the whole range of entrepreneurial skills.

Like all entrepreneurs they must be well-informed. They must read widely and monitor the mass media. They must do their research, building up a detailed picture of the social classes, the industries, the services, the pastimes and problems of their areas. They must get to know the way people live and develop a 'feel' for their concerns and interests. They must keep abreast of developments in their own profession, and keep an eagle eye on what their competitors for the leisure-time of their potential students are doing.

Like all entrepreneurs they must always be on the lookout for new ideas and people. Heads of established centres will regularly receive letters from would-be tutors offering art, sociology, rock-music, dolly-bird dressmaking, animated film-making, aikido, parapsychology, woodcarving.... They will receive unsolicited visits from would-be tutors who have worked up a pre-packaged course on their particular hobby-horse and are touting it around—a recently retired business-man, for example, who has prepared a ten-lecture course on

'Making Meaningful Managerial Decisions' or a postgraduate architecture student who wants to make some pocket money by passing on some of the information she is researching. Here the analogy is with the old-time theatrical entrepreneur, sitting in his office talking to ideas men, reading scripts, and auditioning a whole variety of artistes from the grand actor to the vaudeville fire eater. Adult educators, too, need a 'nose' for a good idea and must be shrewd judges of talent.

Like all entrepreneurs, they must be innovators themselves. And when they do hit upon an idea they must be prepared to take risks. At Addison some of the failures included 'Consumer Education', 'Structure Construction', and a multi-media arts and crafts ticket that enabled students to pop into various arts and crafts classes in rotation. A high-risk success was a course on fly-tying. Who would have thought there would be enough anglers living in an inner city area to come to a course that taught the delicate and time-consuming art of making anglers' flies? The vice-principal did. And he was right.

And having set up their programme, adult educators must be able to 'sell' it. Like entrepreneurs, they must be publicists.

Wheeler-dealer
Adult educators must be wheeler-dealers, hustlers on behalf of the communities they serve. They need boundless energy. Listen to the principal of Frobisher Institute, an adult education centre in south-east London:

We're involved in all sorts of things. Up by the river for example. All those docks, all those warehouses, the whole area due for redevelopment. We're not going to let them pull it all down and put up another concrete city. We want to keep some of our heritage, move in some local craftsmen, set up community workshops, get arts and crafts centres going, make the place available for small local industries. . . . I'm involved in contracts, leasing premises, petitioning, getting planning permission. I sometimes wonder whether all this is adult education. I think it is . . .

I had some trouble getting a class for Turkish mothers off the ground. In my opinion they were such an isolated group that if we were going to teach them English from scratch we really needed someone who spoke Turkish to do the job. I found a woman who was good enough to go up and down the country acting as an English-Turkish interpreter in the courts but she wasn't on the panel of approved language teachers. For some reason County Hall dragged their feet and I couldn't pay her. So we started the class and I paid her as a part-time male assistant—a handyman—and to top that up so that she got something like the full tutor's fee the school we were running the project with paid her as a play-ground supervisor . . . .

With all the cutbacks and lack of funds we've linked ourselves with a number of local organisations and gone looking for money from other sources. We've got grants from various places and attracted a lot of urban aid. We've looked for premises we don't have to pay for and used staff paid by someone else. In a period of no growth we've increased the adult education provision in the area by 6,000 tutor hours a year. It doesn't matter who's paying. It's still adult education . . . .

Administrator
Frobisher Institute runs over 700 classes a week in an extra-ordinary range of places including schools, clinics, community centres, settlements, factories, old people's homes, hospitals, halls, borough day centres, youth centres, a psychiatric centre and a bus. If you take into account all the sites, then Frobisher operates on something like seventy premises!

The day-to-day running of such an unwieldy organisation is a massive task, involving as it does the supervision of classes and sites, the management of a sizeable recurrent budget, the administering of employment contracts and payment of the part-time staff, the enrolment of several thousand students, the constant shuffling of equipment and resources around the branches, the liaison with local education authority departments for such matters as maintenance and supplies, and the liaison with all the other voluntary and statutory agencies whose premises the institute uses and with whom the institute is administratively linked through joint projects.

Frobisher is a large urban adult education centre, but the challenges are just as great for a rural agency responsible for a wide range of activities taking place in a scatter of villages covering half a county, or for a university extramural department slotting individual courses into the programmes of a large number of other centres and institutions. Adult educators must be skilful administrators.

Manager

Frobisher has approximately 300 part-time tutors. Some teach for other adult education centres, others are teachers or lecturers in the other sectors of the education service and others work in full-time jobs unconnected with education at all.

The institute has seven tutors-in-charge of branches. They, too, are part-timers with other jobs or responsibilities. Then there are the clerical staff, the playroom staff, the canteen staff, the odd-job men and the school guards, all part-time.

All major branches have schoolkeepers. They are full-time, but when a building is shared with a day school they must of necessity have divided loyalties.

The institute has eight full-time educational staff and two full-time support staff. One of the educational staff shares her responsibilities fifty-fifty with another community agency and another has full-time teaching responsibilities. Four are responsible for 'departments' but because there are not enough full-time staff to go round they also assume responsibility for other departments as well. (Thus the head of nautical subjects keeps a weather eye on the institute's drama classes as well.)

On top of the pile come the vice-principal and the principal, who are assisted by and/or answerable to a staff-student association, an academic board and a governing body.

Managing this army of part-timers and people with divided loyalties would be difficult enough if the institute's programme were reasonably stable and unchanging, but of course it is not. Classes fluctuate in attendance, some close, some open. Community interests change and fashions come and go. Policy at local and central government level shifts in emphasis.

Adult educators have to forge their dispersed and disparate

organisations into coherent structures that can function efficiently and yet maintain the large degree of flexibility necessary to respond to community requirements.[13] To do this they must be good managers.

Animateur

Adult educators must be able to make often grim and forbidding environments into convivial centres. To do this they might suggest meetings between classes engaged in complementary activities. They might encourage arts and crafts classes to mount exhibitions, or the archaeology group to display their finds with a couple of pieces of carefully labelled modern plastic drain piping thrown in amongst the Roman shards for the fun of it. They might invite the rock music class to meet the classical music appreciation class for a public debate. They might persuade the cinema tutor to screen a nasty excerpt from the original *Frankenstein* film one evening in the canteen during break. They might encourage the badminton group to challenge a neighbouring centre to a match, or help the Spanish tutors organise an intensive residential weekend for the Spanish classes at a conference centre somewhere in the country.

Adult Educators must have that almost magical ability to bring the right people and the right resources together at the right time in order to make things happen. They must be *animateurs*.

Troubleshooter

In an organisation with all these people and all these activities something is bound to go wrong. A tutor rings two minutes before his class is due to start to say that his car has broken down on the flyover. The heating goes haywire. An elderly student faints in the canteen. The word 'fuck' appears on one of the children's drawings on display in one of the classrooms and the infants school head is out and about looking for blood. Three long-legged young women walk into a branch with some story about one of the tutors promising them jobs in Barcelona. The tutor is nowhere to be seen. The religious studies inspector calls in from one of the outlying branches. He is a mild man but obviously ropeable. He has come all the way across town to sits in on a course called 'Religion and Society in Crisis' which the centre closed down two weeks ago because of lack of response. A student complains that the art tutor is giving her less time than he is giving the other students in the class. A wallet is reported stolen. The centre's best French tutor is pregnant again. A local councillor hears about a course called 'Strikes and Strife in Industry' and complains that ratepayers' money is being spent down at the local centre to foment revolution.

Running an adult education centre requires skill in crisis management. Adult educators must be cool, calm, and collected troubleshooters.

I know a troubleshooter *par excellence*. He has the right background for it. He went through Dunkirk, then to Cairo with the Royal Army Service Corps where he ran a massive repair depot for lorries, tanks, cranes and anything else mechanical that could be made to move again, employing an Egyptian labour force supplemented with Italian prisoners of war. He worked on the wreckage of battles and campaigns right across North Africa and up to Turkey. After the war he went into the motor industry ending up as the director of a large branch of a large motor car distributor. He had always worked as a part-time tutor and/or administrator in further and then adult education, and in his fifties he moved over to adult education full-time. He has a wealth of practical, useful information at his fingertips and is used as a source of considered advice by virtually everyone who knows him. His years in the world of hard knocks and tough commercial competition show in the superb skill with which he can soothe a ruffled student, keep warring tutors apart, repair a breakdown in the logistics of the centre, and get part-time and full-time staff (including his superiors) moving quickly to sort out some administrative tangle. But then, any problem adult education can throw up must be child's play after North Africa.

Expert on Method
And of course adult educators must be educators. They must be educational Jacks-of-all-trades, capable of advising the Russian tutor one moment and guiding the 'Cake Decoration

and Confectionery' class through a rough patch the next. This may seem the tallest of a lot of tall orders, but in fact adult educators are in an unrivalled position to see tutors in all sorts of subjects in action, to observe how groups of adults respond to different techniques in different disciplines, and to gain an insight into all the subtle forces that come into play in an adult classroom. The full-time staff at Addison, for example, have more than 500 classes to visit, observe and draw conclusions from. Adult educators will be unable to gain any but the most superficial knowledge of most of the subjects in their pro-grammes but they have the most extraordinary opportunity to make themselves experts in *method*.

And expert advice on method can be the most important thing adult educators have to offer. Often accommodation is poor and resources are limited, but if adult educators can make the activities they are responsible for 'hum' then that is worth any number of purpose-built centres and any amount of first-class equipment.

Campaigner
Finally, adult education is always under threat. It is under threat from its political masters who all too often have very little idea of its function or value.[14] It is under threat from people in the other sectors of the education service, some resenting the resources adult education diverts from the sacrosanct business of getting pupils and students through their exams, and others seeing adult education as nothing more than a noisome night intruder on their precious day-school premises.[15] And it is under threat even from within its own ranks from certain adult educators who try to ape the practices of the other sectors, and so deny adult education its unique and fundamentally different character.

As a result, adult educators must believe in adult education and be prepared to do battle for what they believe in.

Chapter 12

Leisure Learning in Action

I would like to end this part of the book by describing three examples of leisure learning in action. They come from a period fairly early on in my adult education career when I was both the tutor of a creative writing class and the tutor-in-charge of a branch of a centre. The branch was a large secondary school during the day and a colourless, characterless place in the evenings, and when I was appointed tutor-in-charge I tried to liven the place up by getting the art classes to mount an exhibition, playing records during tea-break, and setting up a notice board for use by students. I also set about arranging meetings between classes that I felt might be able to collaborate usefully. Of these attempts to couple classes, one was a success, another a failure and a third I am still not sure about . . . .

The Success
This coupling of classes was unremarkable in itself but set in motion a train of events that ended up a year or so later with some of the local clergy protesting and a photo in a national Sunday newspaper. The two classes were my writing class and the drama class. The groups met one evening to discuss some of the problems of writing for the stage and to watch the drama group perform two scenes from a play they were working on. The only immediate result of the meeting was that I lost one of my students. He had been trying to write television plays and I and the group had not been of any great help, so when we met the drama group he defected. He did not act, but sat about at the back of the hall during the

drama group's meetings gradually putting a play together. The drama tutor worked with him away from the branch and together they began to construct a workable piece of theatre.

Wearing my tutor-in-charge hat I encouraged the group to put on a semi-public performance of the play in the upstairs hall. The play made use of the Christmas story and the aim was to perform it in the last week before the Christmas break, but the production was not ready and with a little rewriting our sights were re-set on the week before Easter. This time the play did take place. The centre hired some stage lighting, organised tickets and publicity, invited the local press and to everyone's gratification attracted quite a sizeable audience.

The play was about abortion. A young woman is pregnant and she and her boyfriend encounter prejudice, anger, fear, ignorance and self-interest in those around them. Throughout the play parallels are drawn with the Christmas story. The young woman is seen as the Virgin Mary in the opening scene and, as the play progresses and the pressure on the couple to abort the child grows, reference is continually made to the Christmas story in separate scenes and in background music consisting almost entirely of carols.

In the final scene — the abortion scene — the play returned to the opening tableau of the Virgin and Child. The three wise men entered, hooded and cloaked, and knelt around the child; and I watched with mild interest, lulled by the carols perhaps, as they went through the ritual motions of obeisance before the manger. The dénouement, when it came, was very neatly done. I was caught totally unprepared and, judging from the audible reaction in the hall, so were the rest of the audience. Up to this point the modern story and the Christmas story had remained separate. Now in an instant they elided. The three wise men flicked off their hoods to reveal themselves as the woman's father, a priest from an earlier scene and the boyfriend, drew long knives from their cloaks, and in perfect unison raised and plunged the knives into the manger. It was one of those moments. Three sharp movements and the knives were raised. Infinitesimal pause, then down.

The next edition of the local newspaper carried a quintessential piece of local journalism. The story appeared under the headline SCHOOL HALL DEATH PLAY and carried a photo of the descent of the knives, but it was not so much about the play as about a couple of local clergymen's reactions to it. 'The whole idea of this production is horrible', one was quoted as saying. The other used the word 'blasphemous' and said he would not allow anyone to present a play of this sort in his church hall. Needless to say, no one had asked him to. This story was picked up in its turn by the *Sunday People* and printed with the same photo and clergymen's comments, this time under the more heart-rending headline BABY JESUS KNIFED IN SHOCK PLAY.

When the dust settled we were left with a student who had written and seen his own full-length play performed, a drama group who had gone through the complex business of rehearsing and mounting an original production, and an adult education centre which had gained some nationwide publicity.

The Failure

In the case of the writing group and drama group all I did was arrange the first meeting. From then on events took their own course. In this next case, however, I planned the whole project.

The idea was to hold a fashion show of outfits made by the members of several dressmaking classes, and to have it compèred by members of the 'Communications and Public Speaking' class. I approached the tutors and they agreed. My plan was to do the thing in reasonable style—soft music on the record player, duplicated programme notes, the canteen lit by spotlights following the 'models' as they walked along a catwalk of tables amidst all the people from the other classes taking their tea-break. My hope was that the event would give the dressmaking classes something to work together for, and that the 'Communications and Public Speaking' class would enjoy themselves over a few meetings working out descriptions to go with the outfits and putting together a fifteen-minute commentary which could be shared between several of them.

We set a date and all appeared to go well for several weeks with the dressmakers enthusiastically preparing their collections and a silence from the 'Communications and Public Speaking' group that I assumed betokened industrious preparation. A week from the day while I was in the midst of planning the catwalk with a dressmaking tutor, the tutor of the 'Communications and Public Speaking' group approached me. She told me her class was sadly depleted in numbers and that those that remained did not want to take part in the event. She did not say so in so many words but I realised that my scheme had almost killed her class off. Rather than face the difficult job of refusing to co-operate, those students who were not attracted by the idea of compèring a fashion show or were daunted by the prospect or annoyed by my intrusion into the affairs of their group had chosen adult education's time-honoured way of registering their lack of interest, timidity or anger and had stayed away. The tutor had found herself with her course programme seriously interrupted and most of her class missing.

I broke the news to the dressmakers. We discussed the possibility of getting someone else to do the commentary but it was decided that that would not be the same thing. I did not press the matter and friends and husbands were told not to come, the dressmakers showed their dresses to each other in the dressmaking room, and the non-event slipped into the past.

I visited the 'Communications and Public Speaking' class a couple of weeks later and as I sat and listened, it all became too painfully obvious. The course was not on the finer points of public oratory at all. It was about basic language skills, about talking to each other, about overcoming one's diffidence in the presence of others. One student had a stammer. Two spoke English well enough but certainly not as their mother tongue. One man had come along to learn how to present himself more effectively in interview. Others were there because they wanted practice in the very ordinary conversational forms that come naturally to most of us but that they found difficult. The tutor was extraordinarily clever at finding ways to bring together this diverse group of people in a variety of language exercises and role play so that they not only tackled their individual concerns but also engaged in quite a profound examination of language, meaning and social relationships.

And how had I come to meddle in such a delicately organised activity? The answer is simple, of course. Through ignorance.

The Doubtful One

This third coupling of classes involved a first-year Italian class and a cookery class. My suggestion was that they combine for an Italian evening with the cookery tutor supervising the cooking of an Italian meal and the Italian tutor giving a language class based on expressions needed in the kitchen and restaurant. The cost of the food would be borne equally by the two classes, and at the end of the lesson they would all sit down and enjoy the meal together. I had not imagined that there would be any difficulty in implementing my suggestion, but, unlike Jeeves, I had failed to take into account the psychology of the individuals involved.

The Italian tutor was very Italian. He taught only one evening a week and once I asked him why he did it. 'I like it' he said with an expansive gesture to underline how obvious the answer was.

The cookery tutor was English. She was also an excellent and dedicated tutor and not terribly enthusiastic when I approached her about the combined evening with the Italian class. 'I have a lot still to get through', she said, looking worried. I argued that the evening would be enjoyable and that it would not be wasted since she would have to instruct her class in the dishes for the dinner in any event. She said she had not intended teaching an Italian dish and that she would have to think it over.

The Italian tutor was immediately enthusiastic about the idea, and so was his class. I told them that the cookery class was not yet convinced.

'Tell them', the Italian tutor said, 'that *we* will bring the wine.'

I reported this to the cookery class but the tutor and most of the class still looked dubious. I reported back to the Italian tutor. 'They aren't really very keen on cooking an Italian dish', I said.

'Tell them', the Italian tutor said, 'that *I* will cook the dish.'

I told the cookery tutor that she could let the Italian tutor cook the dish. She told me that her group were not terribly keen on sharing the cost of the food. The dinner was likely to cost them more than they usually allocated for each evening and in any case they normally took home what they had cooked rather than consume it on the centre's premises. I reported back to the Italian tutor. He looked at me for a moment.

"Tell them', he said, 'that *I* will provide the food!'

I conducted the Italian tutor down to the cookery class so that he could announce this himself. He walked in, greeted the class as if they were old friends and said: 'We will have a wonderful dinner together. I will cook some wonderful Italian dishes and we will eat and drink together.'

The cookery class was largely unresponsive. One or two people nodded. The Italian tutor said: 'Good'. He turned to the cookery tutor. 'You have the salt?' he asked

'Ah . . . well, not really' she said. 'You see normally each of us —'

For the first time the Italian tutor looked anything but his flamboyantly cheerful self. 'It doesn't matter,' he said darkly, '*I* will bring the salt.'

He walked out and I followed him. In the corridor he said: 'They do not even offer to bring the salt!' I assured him the cookery tutor had not meant that; that her class's apparent lack of enthusiasm was simply an example of that English habit of resisting overtures of friendship; and that the evening would be a great success. He looked dubious but agreed to go ahead.

But I had been worried by the cookery class's response as well, and I went back into the cookery room. 'You do realise that he will be providing everything himself,' I said. 'It should be a very enjoyable evening.'

The class looked at me.

'You *are* going to come, aren't you?' I said.

Everyone nodded or said 'yes', but even then something made me doubt them and I made one last effort to elicit some sign of enthusiasm.

'Do you know that the Italian tutor has an interest in a number of hotels and is', I said, lying in my teeth, 'a qualified and experienced chef?'

'Oh,' said one of the class, 'then perhaps I *will* come.'

The evening itself was a great success. The Italian tutor brought the food, which he said he had got cheap through some hotelier contacts. The Italian class turned up with a lot of wine. The Italian tutor cooked with a lot of flourish and some expertise; and talked entertainingly as he did it. A reasonable number of the cookery class turned up. The Italian tutor had brought along a friend to bolster the number of men. The friend was tall, young, handsome and, in his fisherman's cap and fisherman's heavy-knit jumper, Italian to the point of parody. Someone brought along a collection of Italian pop records. One or two of the cookery class became very red in the face from the wine and within minutes of sitting down to the meal the tutor's friend seemed well on the way to cementing a relationship with one of the sexier-looking members of the Italian class. There was a lot of laughter. The evening may not have marked a great stride forward in the programmes of either class but it did make the point that it is pleasant to eat good food in the company of others.

One of the members of the cookery class said to me afterwards: 'That was fun. We must do it again.'

Relevance

In my attempts to liven up the branch I realise now that I was harking back to my experience as a university student. In addition to completing a fairly broad arts degree, I engaged in a number of extra-curricular activities—singing in the choir, acting with the university dramatic society, and so on. Having been through this kind of educational experience I assumed without any reflection that people in any educational context would want to meet and that nothing but good could come of mixing disciplines.

But adult education is different. University provides a student with a protracted period of three or so years in an artificial context where people of differing interests are able to meet whether there is any immediately recognisable reason for doing so or not. The adult education student, on the other hand, walks into an adult education centre out of his own real life. He has made a decision to attend a particular class and will demand of it a relevance that the university student may not demand, and may even be taught *not* to demand.

For the Italian class, meeting the cookery class had a meaning. They were learning a language and the dinner provided them with an opportunity to practise it in another setting, a more relaxed and realistic one than the classroom, in fact. But for the cookery class, learning a few Italian words and cooking a dish not on the programme they and their tutor had mapped out at the beginning of the year must have seemed thoroughly pointless. And although it may have been fun, that was not what they had enrolled for. They had enrolled to learn certain skills in cooking.

But there is another, more important, reason for my disquiet about the Italian dinner. In a way I am still glad that I got that cookery class to unbend a little and enjoy themselves, but I am far from happy about having forced them to do it. *That* is not in the spirit of adult education at all.

PART III
Change

Chapter 13

The Introduction of Salads

A Conference

At a conference in West London in 1974 on a report entitled 'An Education Service for the Whole Community' it became increasingly obvious that of all the educational institutions represented there only the adult education centre—Addison again—operated according to principles that were genuinely comprehensive and community-based. Each of the other sectors—infants, junior, secondary, further education and the youth service—saw its role as providing a clearly defined service for a limited sector of the community. Addison, on the other hand, could point to its standard provision of several hundred classes a week in languages, liberal studies, arts and crafts, sports and hobbies; its classes for parents and pre-school-age children; its language classes for immigrants; its classes and activities for the elderly; its classes for the handicapped; its literacy provision; its educational back-up for local amenity and action groups; and its programme of 'special studies' in which efforts were being made to extend existing subject areas and experiment with course structure, resulting in courses and study groups on 'Cartoon and Comic Strip Design', 'Whole Foods', 'Women and Men', 'Man and his Planet', 'Censorship', 'Flashpoints of the Twentieth Century', and horror movies, to list some of the courses already mentioned.

And yet only five years earlier the institute had boasted nothing but the most conventional provision of courses in hobbies and home interests, grey corridors, a student body unrepresentative of the community at large, and a concept of

response to community requirements symbolised in the attitude of the canteen lady at the headquarters branch to the
provision of bread rolls. This 72-year-old lady bought six
bread rolls each day on her way to the centre and on arrival
very carefully buttered them and filled each one with a slice of
cheddar cheese. Two were reserved for the principal and the
other four were placed on display in a glass case as the only
food the canteen provided for the two or three hundred people
who came to the branch each evening. Once the four rolls were
gone that was it. And if you remonstrated, 'I never do more
than four' she would say.

'But why?' you would ask.

'Because I never sell more than four' she would reply.

Shift in Emphasis

Addison is in no way unique but simply mirrors the changes
adult education underwent in the first half of the 1970s. There
was a shift in emphasis and an increase in provision. Adult
education centres in many parts of the country began adopting
a broader 'community' role, providing support for sometimes
quite radical community activity. Nor was this shift limited to
one agency. In Bristol it was the WEA that led the way in
developing courses related to local issues. In Sheffield the
university developed a series of courses on 'rights' education. In
London the shift began with the local authorities—in the
Hounslow department of adult education, under the aegis of
the further education college in Harrow, and in a number of
ILEA institutes. And in Liverpool all three major agencies—
the WEA, the university and the local authority—worked
towards an adult education provision more meaningful to
working-class communities in specific areas of the city.

As part of this shift in emphasis a new breed of adult
educator began appearing, variously described as community-
orientated lecturers, outreach workers, community education
officers, COBs (community-orientated briefs), and catalysts.

'Outreach worker' seems gradually to have gained general
currency, and despite having a definite moon-base feel to it, it
does manage to catch something of the new emphasis, this new
direction adult education was taking. Adult education was
reaching out, seeking ways of contacting organisations,

individuals, community and social groups that did not make use of adult education but might if provision were made on their home ground and more on their own terms.

Changes in Character
Not unnaturally this shift in philosophy and provision off premises was usually matched by changes in character on premises. Compare the Tuesday evening programmes at the Mary Boon branch of Addison in the following two years:

1970-1	*1974-5*
Classical guitar	Astrology
Cooking for all	Cooking for all
Dressmaking	Conversational English
Fencing	Drawing and painting
French	Dressmaking
Millinery	French (stage two)
Poise, dress and beauty	French (*La France*
culture	*Contemporaine*)
Portuguese	German reading
Tailoring	Millinery
	Mental illness
	Patisserie, cakes and bread
	Portuguese (stage one)
	Tailoring
	West Indian drama
	Women's liberation
	Yoga

—and imagine the change in character of the queue in the canteen at tea break and in the general atmosphere of the branch as a result of the influx of new and different people.

Or walk into the Allfarthing branch of Central Wandsworth Adult Education Institute on a Friday and see their family workshop in session. The Allfarthing centre is the top floor of a building otherwise occupied by a school and up till 1969 here on Fridays the institute ran a small number of traditional classes. Now when you enter you are met by the sight of adults and children engaged in what appears to be one large open-plan session of playing and learning. It is a colourful, attractive, seductive scene, for if you do not immediately join in yourself you will be drawn in by a child or adult who needs your help in whatever they are doing. The whole floor is given over to the workshop. There is no strict division between activities, or rigid hours. The large hall is used as a central meeting place and canteen where people can sit and chat, drink coffee or tea, and engage in a number of craft activities that do not need specialised equipment. Opening off this central hall are a number of rooms where more specialised crafts and activities take place. There are tutors available to advise and instruct, but since the whole workshop is based on exchange and mutual help they are sometimes difficult to pick out. There is a crèche for the very young and a playgroup for the under-fives, so that adults and children can be together or apart, playing, experimenting, discovering and learning.[16]

And if this is not enough, go back to Addison headquarters branch where, as a result of the pressure brought to bear by the recently formed students' association, the canteen lady finally gave way and in 1974-5 the canteen began offering salads.

Chapter 14

Four Courses

New subjects, new people, children as well as adults, experiments in form and structure, a shift to a more active, sometimes radical, community role; and all this in a period of less than five years. How did it come about?

Origins

The temptation is to point to adult education's origins in the last century and beyond[17] and say that adult education had gone full circle. After all, adult education in Britain in the nineteenth century was concerned with the central issues of people's lives, not their leisure pursuits. It was concerned with rights, with people educating themselves so that they could represent themselves more fairly in the fields of employment and politics. Working-class men and women came together to learn to read and write, to study technical subjects, and to study and discuss history, politics and economics. And many of the early adult education centres were 'community based', in that they fostered the idea of self-help and responded to local conditions and needs. In the twentieth century, as local authorities took up adult education, there was a major shift away from this kind of provision to the provision of hobbies and interests; and some community educators might be inclined to write off the dressmaking and pottery period of the 1950s and 1960s in particular as a period of aberration from which the service is only now showing fitful signs of recovery.

Yet paradoxically it was during this period of 'aberration' that the principles and practices were established that permitted radical developments to take place. For it was in this period when the provision was exclusively non-vocational that adult education learnt uncomplicatedly to respond to demand, opening and closing classes as interests waxed and waned. It was in this period that adult education adopted the eminently practical criteria when appointing tutors of whether they knew the subject from personal practical experience and could get it over, rather than whether they were officially qualified to do so. And it was in this period that adult education adopted its *laissez-faire* attitude to course design, letting the group of adults assembled run the course in the way they wanted, for as long as they wanted, and in the direction they wanted. It was in this period when the pressure was off and the provision anything but controversial that the freedoms peculiar to adult education were able, quietly and largely unnoticed, to flourish; with the result that when pressure was brought to bear on the adult education service to respond to social and community changes taking place in the late 1960s and early 1970s, as much to its own surprise as anyone else's, adult education found that it could.

Here are four examples of the way in which adult education made that response.

Welfare Rights at Bethnal Green Institute

The end of the 1960s was a period of growing belief in community action. Several free schools came into being. Local residents' groups began opposing the planners. The idea of neighbourhood councils was being mooted. Claimants unions were appearing. Tenants' associations were becoming active. Agencies involving themselves in direct action in the fields of civil liberties, housing and poverty were coming into being or growing more active. Community activists were on the increase, prying information out of sometimes tight-lipped statutory services and demanding the services as a right and not as a charity.

The welfare services—those responsible for assisting and distributing benefits to the unemployed, the ill, the elderly, the handicapped, the homeless and those on low income—came under scrutiny. Various action groups and voluntary agencies gathered together information on the inner workings of the statutory bodies in these fields, on the rules and regulations they applied in distributing benefits, on the criteria both official and unofficial that they used when deciding whether an applicant would receive benefits or not, and on the methods of appeal. They began pointing out anomalies and taking test cases through appeal tribunals in order to correct these anomalies and bring attention to cases where benefits appeared to have been unjustly withheld.

As the body of information gathered by these groups grew, so did the need for information exchange and training; and in early 1971 two activists[18] working with Islington Poverty Action Group and Hackney Citizens Rights respectively designed a series of meetings under the title 'Welfare Rights Advocacy Course' which they ran in conjunction with Child Poverty Action Group in London, starting in February. There was an enormous response to these meetings—over 200 applicants in the first week after a mention in a national paper—and the two organisers immediately began casting around for suitable sponsors for similar courses. The CPAG meetings had been attended by 'professionals'—social workers, community workers, community activists—and the organisers wanted this time to run a course in a place open to the public and to which local people regularly came.

An adult education institute seemed the logical place and through an ILEA inspector they approached the principals of two institutes. But although the logic may have been apparent to the two activists it was not to the two principals, who declined to help. However, the activists persisted and again with the help of the inspector met the principal of a third institute, this time in the Bethnal Green area of London's East End.

Bethnal Green Institute serves an inner city area that is uniformly working-class. Less than 1 per cent of the population can be classified as professional, and there is no middle-class enclave to be found within the institute's borders that could be used by a cynic to explain away the high attendance at many of its classes. The area is predominantly one of council housing, and traditionally has a high immigrant population. One building in the area started life as a Huguenot church, became a Jewish synagogue and is now a mosque. And it is an area with an elderly population, caused by the movement of the young out of London to new towns.

Because of the nature of the community it serves, the institute has never been able to rely on a 'standard' programme of courses but has always been obliged to confer with members of the community and representatives of local organisations and agencies to find the right kind of provision. Over the years Bethnal Green Institute has earned a reputation for enthusiastic community involvement.

The principal agreed immediately to sponsor the course. The activists first approached the institute in early April 1971 and by mid-April, less than three weeks later, the course was under way. The activists provided the speakers and the institute administered and funded the course, paying the speakers and slotting the course into a regular programme of activities it ran at Hoxton Hall, a Quaker settlement in the area.

The course was called 'Citizens' Rights'. It consisted of twelve meetings and covered an enormous range of subjects:

Housing the varying rights to security of furnished, unfurnished and council/housing association tenants; how to get repairs done; rent fixing procedures; tactics against harassment and illegal evictions; redevelopment and rights to compensation and/or rehousing; participation in planning; leasehold reform.

Social security pension rights, unemployment and sickness benefits; supplementary benefits; special allowances.

Denials of entitlement wage stop, rent stop, 'work shy' rulings, accusations of cohabitation; how to fight these denials.

Tribunals supplementary benefits appeals, National Insurance tribunals, rent tribunals; their power, procedures, range of evidence, use of codes and case law.

Other allowances and benefits rent and rate rebates; education benefits; local authority provisions for the old, the disabled, etc.

Civil rights legal aid and advice services; basic rights on arrest and in court.

The speakers on the course included lawyers, university lec-turers, social and community workers and journalists and they were all associated with action and pressure groups such as CPAG, the Citizens Rights Office, Hackney Citizens Rights Group, the National Council for Civil Liberties, and residents' action groups. About fifty people came to the first meeting but as the course continued attendance settled down to about thirty each evening. They were a mix of local people, community activists and professional community and social workers.

It was decided to repeat the course in the next term and in all the institute ran the course four times over a period of about a year, each time attracting good attendances and an increasing number of local people. In the later courses a local element was introduced and one or two officers from local branches of the statutory agencies were invited along, not only to speak on the workings of their agencies but also to answer such basic questions as: 'Why are the windows at your offices so low that the client has to stoop to speak to the person behind the counter?'

Since this course was one of the first of its kind it rated a mention in several magazines and newspapers. Two days after the first meeting in April the London *Evening News* carried a story in which it said:

> [The course] is intended to train people involved in local poverty action groups, tenants associations and other organi-sations to act as 'rights advocates'. They would then be equipped to give advice and represent people who need help or who are worried about benefits, entitlements or rights through lack of knowledge or official action.

The story goes that a senior officer in ILEA was summoned from his office in County Hall to the office of a *very* senior officer. The very senior officer had the item from the *Evening News* on his desk.

'What are you doing at Bethnal Green?' he asked his subordinate. 'Training revolutionaries?'

'Yes,' said the other.

There was a pause while the more senior of the two absorbed this reply, then he murmured: 'I was simply wondering whether the report was true.'

102   *Change*

Alternative Societies at Addison Institute
Through the growing din of the activists in the early seventies
could still be heard the earnest shouts of those in search of an
alternative culture. Flower power was well and truly a thing of
the past and the dust of the student confrontations of 1968 was
settling; parts of the 'movement' had hived off into political
and community action and others such as Women's
Liberation and Gay Liberation had formed coherent movements of their own; but there still remained a sufficient
number of people and underground papers to proclaim that
the search for an alternative society free of ideological hang-
ups was still on. And in 1971 came the final flaring of the
underground flame with the prosecution of three of the
underground's most charismatic figures, the editors of *Oz*, the
London magazine that for five years had been regarded as
almost the official organ of the movement. They were arrested
and brought to trial on several charges to do with allegedly
publishing and distributing pornographic material, all arising
from an issue of the magazine called *Schoolkids Oz*. The trial at
the Old Bailey lasted six weeks. Critics, writers, academics and
educationalists were called as defence witnesses to testify to the
value of the magazine and to comment upon the stands it took
and the ideas it promulgated. One of the editors chose to present
his own defence, making a long and impassioned final speech.

The three were convicted on all but a conspiracy charge.
They were remanded in custody awaiting sentence, during
which period they had their hair forcibly cut. They were all
sentenced to a period in gaol, appealed, were released and
finally had all but one of their convictions quashed. Many of
those who had enjoyed the sixties saw the whole process of
arrest, trial and appeal, which spanned virtually the whole of
1971, as a grand statement of what the underground was (or
had been) about.[19]

Early in that year I introduced Addison's vice-principal to
the editor of *Ink Newspaper*, a recently launched and short-
lived alternative newspaper, and the three of us planned a
course called 'Alternative Societies' for the September term.
This is the course description which appeared in the institute
prospectus for the year 1971-2. It may sound breathlessly
self-important now, but those were heady days:

Around us, perhaps more these days than at any time of history, are the germs of various alternative systems of organising ourselves. A lot of these systems are gathered together under the title 'the Underground', and from this source we are collecting a number of speakers, who will talk about their vision of how our society could be differently run.

It is likely that representatives from the following will take part: Women's Liberation and Freedom Movements, BIT (the underground information service), the Arts Lab Movement, Agit Prop, representatives of both city and rural communes, black communities, Free Communication groups, Black and White Panthers, Yippies, Release (to talk about the role, if any, of drugs), the underground press (various editors who will put forward the philosophies of their papers, e.g. *Oz, It, Friends*, etc.), the underground network (*Vision*), underground film-makers.

We hope to keep the schedule flexible enough to be able to include at the last minute interesting and relevant overseas visitors.

Adult educators are always casting around for ideas for courses that will hit the jackpot, and this one by all conventional standards did. Enrolment for the course was closed at fifty and about another seventy left their names on a waiting list a week ahead of the first meeting. The local press gave it wide coverage and one national, the *Daily Mail*, carried a story about it under the headline UNDERGROUND NIGHT SCHOOL. And at the request of the class the course, originally planned for eleven meetings in the first term, ran on for the whole year and well beyond.

The course followed fairly conventional procedure for most of the first term. The editor of *Ink Newspaper* was employed as the course co-ordinator and each week he invited a guest speaker. The speaker would speak and then there would be discussion. Some of the speakers were as promised in the course blurb. They included one of the *Oz* editors who spoke while on bail pending appeal against his conviction and prison sentence, the organiser of BIT, several other underground journalists and leading figures in the Women's Liberation and Gay

Liberation movements. Other speakers included the director of an arts centre, a television director and a 'radical' barrister.

The group that assembled were extraordinarily varied. The youngest was a seventeen-year-old schoolgirl, who came with her father, and the oldest was seventy-four. The majority were in their twenties or early thirties, but there were at least ten in the over-forty bracket. There were university graduates and people who had left school at the minimum school-leaving age. There were two married couples. Occupations ranged far and wide: male nurse, shopkeeper, fashion designer, X-ray technician, labourer, hotel proprietor, secretary, teacher, mathematician, journalist, photographer. Some dressed conventionally and others wore velvet and beads. There was from the beginning an air of excitement, almost of surprise and suppressed hilarity at actually being in a classroom 'studying' such a subject. This elation reached its peak and communicated itself to the institute principal and the 'parish' inspector who joined the serried ranks of the class on the evening when the *Oz* editor spoke. And the excitement expressed itself in the discussions, which were enthusiastic, involved, at times emotional, and which resulted in at least one walk-out.

About thirty-five of the group asked that the course continue into a second term, and that they play a greater part in the course design themselves. Second term started with a speaker from Recidivists Anonymous on alternatives to prison. During the following week a member of the class visited an RA group meeting in prison and two others visited a self-help hostel set up by RA for recently released members. At the second meeting the class met three ex-prisoners and discussed with them their experiences and suggestions for alternatives to prison. At the third meeting the strands were drawn together in discussion and an informal report. The term continued with the group investigating the case put by Women's Liberation, then People Not Psychiatry. Guests were invited; buzz groups were held, sometimes spreading into several rooms; individuals and groups went out on visits to centres, groups and communes, and on one occasion to join a therapy session based on Reichian methods; and reports and occasional papers were drawn up and circulated.

The group decided to continue into a third term but in an

autonomous form. They chose their own topics, invited their own speakers and organised their own activities, including a weekend away at a conference centre in Oxfordshire. Some of the subjects they discussed were education, environment, sexual mores, and meditative and dietary disciplines. All the institute did in this final term was provide the room and occasional audio-visual aids, and pay three speakers.

When the third term ended about fifteen of the group continued meeting once a week in a nearby pub for several months. Some worked an allotment. There was talk of forming a housing association. And four or five became founder members of the Hammersmith Welfare Rights Group.

The welfare rights course at Bethnal Green Institute was significant because the institute co-operated with an action group — the publicity put out by the institute stated that it was running the course 'in conjunction with Hackney Citizens Rights'; and because of the speed with which the institute was able to respond to demand the course was approved, housed, publicised and under way in a matter of days. But the course itself was conventional in its structure, consisting as it did of a series of pre-arranged lectures delivered by academically expert speakers.

The 'Alternative Societies' course, however, adopted a far less conventional, far more flexible form. Of course it would be pleasing to say that we had intended all along to let the course develop in the way it did. We did state in the course description that the course would be flexible, but we had really only been thinking in terms of minor changes to a pre-arranged list of speakers. However, by the nature of their life-styles, the speakers proved impossible to pin down to definite dates; and very early on the course co-ordinator was obliged to adopt an entirely improvised style of course design, finding his speakers from one week to the next. He took to announcing the various possibilities at the end of each meeting and asking the group to state their preferences. The group began taking part in the course design, helping the co-ordinator track down his speakers and suggesting subjects and finding speakers themselves. This participation developed into the complete autonomy of the last term. Without intending any more than an experiment in subject-matter, Addison found itself embarked on an experiment in form and course control as well.

Civil Rights at South Lambeth Institute

In the sixties race became an issue, marked by pronouncements by politicians and community leaders, the introduction of immigration controls for Commonwealth citizens, and the passing of the Race Relations Acts of 1965 and 1968. Certain districts of certain cities gained notoriety in the press as places of racial tension. And in keeping with the trend towards self-help in the late sixties and early seventies, some immigrant groups began setting up their own organisations or community centres as ways of affirming their own identities and as a base for representation in the community at large.

In 1972 a number of women associated with one of these organisations in London, a black self-help group called the Brixton Neighbourhood Community Association, approached South Lambeth Adult Education Institute asking for a course on civil rights. The women were concerned about their children's relationship with various statutory authorities and wanted to equip themselves with the necessary information to ensure that they or their children were not discriminated against. The institute agreed, and contacted the National Council for Civil Liberties, who provided one of their officers as the tutor. The course went ahead in October in a room above the shopfront headquarters of the Brixton Neighbourhood Community Association.

Ten meetings were held and some twelve women attended regularly. They were all West Indian, of varying ages, and as was to be expected since it was they who had requested the course, most of them already held strong views. The course started with the basic civil rights issues — police powers, arrest, detention, the courts — but as the meetings progressed the course shifted ground from civil rights to educational issues, concentrating more and more on those areas of education where there was likely to be conflict: choosing a secondary school; equal opportunities in school and further and higher education; schools for the educationally subnormal and the methods employed to allocate children to them; and some of the alternatives to the present educational system. As well as the formal meetings, the group visited a magistrate's court and some a juvenile court as well. Several went the rounds of the schools in the area, reporting back to the group and drawing comparisons. One of the group went to the local education office to see what information they made available, how easily they made it available, and how it matched up to the information the group had gathered themselves. And near the end of the course the group spent an evening at the White Lion Street Free School, Islington, talking to the children and staff.

In all this the institute acted as a co-ordinator, putting people in touch with each other, setting up the course and paying the tutor, but exercising no say in the direction the course should take once it was under way. The institute played the part of a servicing agency responding to demand. In a sense Bethnal Green Institute responded to demand also by supporting the welfare rights course, but in that case the group of activists were really only seeking permission to run their own course under the institute's banner and with institute funding. In Brixton, however, the group of women approached South Lambeth Institute empty-handed and asked the institute to put on a course for them. It was, in fact, as neat an example as you could want of an adult centre responding to demand, working in with a pressure group, and providing educational backing for possible action.

Planning and Community Action at South Lambeth Institute
1972 saw a lot of redevelopment going on in the Lambeth, Brixton and Clapham areas of London and in October a community worker from Clapham approached South Lambeth Institute with the idea of running a series of meetings on planning. Through his work he had come into contact with a number of individuals and groups from areas under compulsory purchase orders and was growing concerned at the lack of say people had in planning decisions that drastically affected their lives. He drew up a rough programme for the course and undertook to tutor it in conjunction with a lecturer from the Central London Polytechnic's School of Planning. The institute agreed and together with the community worker set about publicising the course.

The publicity is interesting since it made no bones about

whose side the course would be on. This is the text of the leaflet
that the institute put out under its own name:

ARE THE PLANNERS WORKING ON YOUR NEIGH-
BOURHOOD?
DO YOU AGREE WITH WHAT THEY ARE DOING?
IF NOT, DO YOU KNOW WHAT TO DO ABOUT IT?

A new evening course will be starting at Effra School in
November, which will be concerned with the impact of
redevelopment on the local area, and with the actions which
people can take to oppose, or otherwise influence these
schemes.

The course will aim to explore how and why planning
decisions are made—for example, why some areas rather
than others are selected for redevelopment. It will then
examine the alternative strategies open to people whose
areas are affected by planning decisions. How are levels of
compensation fixed? On what grounds should a planning
appeal be fought? How can pressure best be brought to bear
on planners and politicians? These and other questions will
be looked at, with particular reference to what is going on in
the Lambeth area, and there will be plenty of opportunity
for discussing specific cases. The course will draw on the
knowledge of experts on planning, as well as the experience
of people who—successfully or otherwise—have opposed
redevelopment schemes in other parts of London.

In addition to the leaflet the organisers had a poster
designed. This was even more unequivocal. It was headed: IS
YOUR NEIGHBOURHOOD THREATENED? and depicted
a large, jowly gent, clad in gentleman's outfit complete with
cufflinks, bow tie and carnation in buttonhole, sporting a
colonel's moustache and a monocle, carrying a sheaf of plans
and with a briefcase bearing the word PLANNING beside
him. He was of giant proportions and towered over a street of
inner city housing, pointing imperiously down at the tiny
faceless figures of a couple with a child and a baby in a pram.
The message was simple and emotive. Bureaucracy, vested
interest, wealth and the ruling class pitted against the small
defenceless ordinary man and his family. At the bottom were

the details of time and place and the words: 'Further information from South Lambeth Institute'.

The meetings were held at a branch of the institute and were
attended by about fifteen people. The group was made up of
representatives from a number of groups from different roads
or areas under threat and several others who were there as
individuals. One of these individuals, 'the lady from Lillieshall
Road', came along simply out of interest, but by the end of the
twelve meetings had formed a residents' action group and was
there as its representative.

The course analysed the planning processes and how to
influence them. It concentrated on strategy and useful information, with the accent on useful. People would come to a
meeting saying: 'This is what has happened in our area since
we last met. What do we do now?'

Another twelve meetings were held starting in February
1973 under the same title of 'Planning and Community Action'
and in the following November a series of six meetings were
held under the title 'Planning in Lambeth' which aimed at
forming a planning study group of local residents to continue
after the course had ended.

The welfare rights course at Bethnal Green Institute was, in
a manner of speaking, a 'standard' course and not specifically
concerned with conditions peculiar to Bethnal Green. The
'Alternative Societies' course could have been housed anywhere. Even the 'Civil Rights' course held at the Brixton
Neighbourhood Community Association, although related in
discussion and research to the local context, was not confined
in basic subject-matter to the Brixton area. But the course on
'Planning and Community Action' was not a general or
standard course at all. In fact its title, until changed for the
third series of meetings, could be said to be misleading since
the course concerned itself always with information and
discussion that would prove of immediate use to local people
concerned with protecting their streets and flats and houses.
Every effort was made at every stage to keep the course topical,
local and immediately relevant.

Influence
I have described these four courses in some detail not because

they were trendsetters — adult education in this country is so fragmented that it would always be unwise to claim anything as a 'first' — but because each is an example of the way in which long-established practices usually associated with leisure-learning activities were being successfully applied to the study of social and community issues.

But I do believe it is true to say that within ILEA these courses were the first of their kind, and that they had some influence on future developments. The 'Alternative Societies' course influenced the style and character of much of the special studies at Addison over the next few years, which in its turn drew comment both adverse and favourable from beyond the institute's boundaries. The 'Planning and Community Action' course served as a model for courses on planning in a number of adult education centres over the next two or three years, while only two years after the 'Citizens' Rights' course at Bethnal Green Institute and a year after the 'Civil Liberties' course at South Lambeth Institute, courses on rights were well on their way to becoming a standard part of any reasonably progressive adult education programme. In September 1973 the education officer of the Cobden Trust, an arm of the National Council for Civil Liberties, compiled a list of the courses on welfare rights and civil liberties, planned by various adult education centres in and around London for 1973-4. There were thirty-two.

Chapter 15

Outreach

In the early seventies, new subjects were beginning to appear in some adult education centres; attempts were being made to capitalise on adult education's particular freedoms and not simply to ape the other sectors of the education service; and it was gradually being realised by a small number of community activists and an increasing number of adult educators that adult education could be drawn much more directly into the fields of community development and action. A shift in style and emphasis was under way.

Another factor in the shift was the introduction of outreach work. In one way outreach work was nothing new. It was a form of community work. But some of the practices of community work put into question conventional educational thinking and for the staid and unimaginative adult education sevice of the fifties and sixties outreach work was revolutionary.

Background
ILEA evidence to the Russell Committee. The introduction of outreach work occurs not surprisingly in a period when adult education was being required to take a look at itself. Its origins in London can probably be found in the evidence ILEA submitted to the Russell Committee on Adult Education. The authority was invited to make the submission in 1969 and as part of the process of compiling the evidence carried out a survey to obtain information on the characteristics of people attending their adult education institutes. The survey found that more women than men attended; that students had a

lower average age than the population of inner London and typically left full-time education later; and that of the students who were employed only 4 per cent were semi-skilled or unskilled manual workers as opposed to 31 per cent of the employed population in inner London.[20]

ILEA working party on the social structure of the student body of adult education institutes. This last finding set ILEA principals and officers wondering, and in 1970, in response to a letter from the principals' association, ILEA set up a working party 'to consider and report to the Education Officer on the reasons for low numbers of unskilled and manual workers enrolling for classes at adult education institutes and to suggest ways in which their interest might be stimulated'.

The working party is significant more because of its existence than because of its conclusions. The figures arrived at in the survey for the evidence to the Russell Committee were cast into doubt by the working party, but it did seem true that adult education in London was not reaching large sectors of the community. The setting up of the working party reflected concern at this, and ILEA began implementing some of the solutions even before the working party had finished analysing the problems. These solutions included an injection of funds and equipment into the institutes, an increase of full-time staff, and the appointment of the first outreach workers. By the time the working party reported in 1973 and made as its first recommendation that 'additional full time teaching staff be appointed to research into the educational needs of the community and for liaison with various statutory and voluntary agencies', outreach workers had been appointed to some six or seven institutes.

But it would be wrong to see the introduction of outreach work in quite such simple and direct terms. There were other factors and influences at play.

ILEA internal report 839. The first proposal for an outreach style of appointment comes not in the report on the social structure of the student body, but in ILEA document 839 which was submitted to the ILEA Further and Higher Education Sub-Committee in February 1970. This document was a review of the adult and youth services and proposed bringing them together in order to provide an integrated non-vocational education service catering for all ages from fourteen upwards. Within this new structure it was proposed to appoint 'education-based field-workers' called 'Education Community Officers' who would be 'the main field worker and link with statutory provision' and play a major part in developing 'lines reaching out into the community at field level'.

The Sub-Committee referred document 839 to a working party whose report entitled *A Chance to Choose* (1972) argued that the youth and adult education services should remain to all intents and purposes separate. ILEA accepted this recommendation and document 839 sank, but not before having provided a thumbnail description for these new types of appointment and having prepared the linguistic ground for the word 'outreach'.

The Liverpool experience. Keith Jackson was the assistant director of the Institute of Extension Studies at Liverpool University at the time of the Educational Priority Area Project in Liverpool during the late sixties and early seventies. Tom Lovett was appointed in 1969 as the WEA tutor-organiser in the Liverpool Education Priority Area. Both men worked through their agencies to bring adult education resources and techniques into this inner city area, whose inhabitants were largely semi-skilled or unskilled working class and where there were high unemployment, low wages and poor housing. Keith Jackson aimed to provide training in the techniques and philosophy of community development for working-class activists, community workers, the clergy, and voluntary and statutory social workers in the area, and so to complement Tom Lovett's more direct action-research with tenants associations and community groups in the field. During 1970 and 1971 both men fired off articles to *Adult Education* and *Studies in Adult Education* recounting their experiences and arguing for a new, committed, community-oriented approach to the provision of adult education. The articles are couched in a style suitable to the professional organs in which they appear, but they are despatches from the front line and one can sense an exhilaration just beneath the surface, and a barely contained irritation at colleagues who cannot see the significance of what they are doing and saying.[21]

Here, for example, in a jointly written article entitled

'Universities and the WEA—an alternative approach', they describe how Tom Lovett went about his job:

> In Liverpool, for instance, the WEA tutor-organiser attached to the Liverpool Educational Priority Area project has initiated or taken part in a wider range of adult 'activities'. These included running an adult education stall in a large department store; assisting residents involved in the Liverpool Shelter Neighbourhood Action Project to draw up *their* plans for *their* neighbourhood; helping residents set up their own community centre; helping run a summer playscheme for parents and children; organising discussion groups on topics of general interest in schools, pubs, community centres, church halls, private homes; conducting a house-to-house survey of adult education needs and then organising activities for those expressing interest; commissioning an EPA show for local residents designed to utilise game playing techniques, in an attempt to examine the education system; helping a local community council to explore the educational needs of its community; and writing and broadcasting a six-week series of programmes of general concern in the EPA.[22]

This article appeared two months before the first outreach worker was appointed in London, and two years before the ILEA working party on the social structure of the adult education student body recommended that such appointments become part of official policy. Indeed, the working party formally recognised the importance of the Liverpool experience in their report, mentioning Tom Lovett by name and stating that they 'have studied with interest the literature concerning the Liverpool Project'.

An initiative by an individual principal.[23] It was no accident that the first outreach worker was appointed to Bethnal Green Institute. The welfare rights course held there brought the principal into contact with community activists and it was at that time that he approached the central authority seeking permission to appoint a full-time member of staff who would concentrate on reaching the non-users. The authority agreed and the first outreach worker, at that stage cumbersomely and inaccurately described as a 'community orientated lecturer', was interviewed and appointed in September 1971. Two more appointments quickly followed, then after a pause of almost a year, three more. From then on appointments were made steadily so that at the beginning of the 1977 - 8 year there were more than twenty full-time staff attached to ILEA institutes who in some way at least could be described as outreach workers.

A Strategy for Change?
There may be a further explanation as to why senior ILEA officers pushed ahead with the appointment of outreach workers even when, as happened on more than one occasion, certain principals resisted the idea. Initially, at least, outreach workers may have been appointed not just to devise provision for sections of the community that seemed to have no use for adult education in its present form, but also to stir up the service itself. Certainly to those principals who were content to see out their few remaining years of service providing a standard programme of hobbies and interests the first few outreach workers must have seemed a rum, and threatening, bunch.

Of the first seven appointed none came from conventional adult education backgrounds and three from outside the education service altogether. One had worked in a senior post in the voluntary sector of social services. Another had been a minister of religion with several years' association with student movements, and was an enthusiastic and original advocate of the thinking of the Latin-American educationalist, Paulo Freire. Another was trained as an economist and had worked as a research officer for one of the large trade unions. Another had worked in further education setting up courses in language for the Asian community in Leicester and running a radio programme. Another had taught in a large prison and had run the education department in a smaller prison. Another was a sociologist, trained into a fascinated interest in the inner city but torn by his desire to retreat to a rural commune in Scotland. And I had been a journalist, then briefly an actor, then a part-time teacher of English as a foreign language.

We operated with extraordinary freedom. Although we had

been appointed to each institute below the principal and vice-principal, no one really knew what we were meant to do . . . nor often enough where we were. One outreach worker rang up another institute and asked for her counterpart.

'He's not in' came the reply.

'Do you know where he is?' asked the outreach worker.

'Yes' came the reply. 'He's out in the community.'

As a result of this freedom and the differing conditions from one institute to another, the ways in which outreach workers set about their jobs varied enormously. At Addison I set about broadcasting the existence of the institute and the fact that it was there to be used by groups involved in community development and action, and set up a programme of 'special studies' in an attempt to prove it. At Central London Institute the worker saw the opportunity for creating a crafts centre and devoted a lot of her energy to setting this up in a way that would allow the users control over the activities the institute supported there. In North Kensington the outreach worker quickly abandoned on-premises courses and threw himself into the affairs of the community, advertising the existence of the institute but beyond that seeing his experience and support, his constant questioning and listening, as the best contribution he could make to learning situations as and where they arose. At one end of the spectrum there would be a formal course called 'Community Self-Help' and at the other end the worker participating in the setting up of a builders' co-operative and negotiating work for the co-operative with a housing association. And yet despite the fact that no two outreach workers went about their jobs in exactly the same way, a certain style and common attitude did develop quickly. And certain areas of activity became recognised as unquestionably outreach work.

Non-users

Most outreach workers saw their first priority as being to identify various sections of the community that did not use adult education, to make contact and investigate with them ways in which adult education might offer support. Several outreach workers identified housing estates from which their institutes drew very few students and made approaches to see whether any other form of provision was wanted. The approach might be made through the tenants' association if one existed, with the help and advice of community workers if they existed, through statutory officers of one sort or another, or simply by making contact with individuals and small groups in places like the local laundrette or café or community hall. The end result might be a keep-fit class in a community hall, a mothers and babies club, a crafts group, or a weekly discussion group to which the various local government officers having responsibility for the affairs of the estate and its locality were invited.

To a traditionalist such discussion groups might seem too far removed from the structured course in which a group of students are led step by step towards a clear set of educational goals. He might argue that this sort of meeting was more appropriately the province of the community worker or local political activist. But it was precisely these distinctions that outreach work was blurring. The outreach worker might reply that if there was a chance of constructive learning taking place, then he had every justification for being involved. And there is no doubt that in meetings where responsible officers and community groups meet each other a lot of learning can take place on both sides. The members of one such discussion group on an estate with a reputation for violence went away deep in thought from an evening spent in discussion with the police officers whose beat covered the estate. They had been told that the crime rate and incidence of violence on the estate were no higher than the norm for that police division.

What was wrong? Who was wrong? Was the police definition of violence not the same as that accepted by the tenants on the estate? Or had the notoriety of the estate been based on isolated incidents and simply fed on fear? Was there even a deliberate policy of scaremongering? How could the police who patrolled there and the people who lived there have such different assessments of something so simple and obvious as violence? Was violence simple and obvious? Perhaps living on the edge of violence in a state of fear and suspicion becomes indistinguishable from being caught in the midst of the physical manifestation of violence.

The adult educator who organised these meetings was an action/research worker attached to the Department of

Extra-Mural Studies of the University of London and he had one or two sceptics among his colleagues back in the department's central London headquarters. In this case he was able to satisfy their traditionalist requirements by pointing to the fact that after a couple of years his discussion group formed a small study group and embarked on a quite formal course on local history. But where they might see the local history course as a justification of his involvement, he would have seen it simply as a welcome by-product of an already thoroughly educational activity.[24]

Of course, in terms of actual classes, the result of an outreach worker's approach to an estate might, after months of hard work, be nothing.

Several outreach workers took English classes to immigrant groups on their own territory or at their place of work. An example of this was an English class I took in a large commercial laundry where many of the workers were Asian. The class started half an hour before the morning shift and extended fifteen minutes, twenty minutes, twenty-five minutes — until the foreman finally lost patience — into the firm's time. This trial of strength between the group and the foreman gave the last few minutes of each meeting an element of excitement not always found in the English classes back at the institute.

Other outreach workers attempted to increase the provision for the elderly, organising meetings on pensioners' rights, increasing the number of leisure learning activities specifically aimed at the elderly, and organising oral history projects in which a group of pensioners might make a tape recording of their memories of the area they lived in. One outreach worker organised a general education class on a gypsy camp-site, using a play-bus as the classroom. Several outreach workers devoted a large amount of their time to setting up provision for parents of pre-school-age children, which also meant considering provision for the children as well. New courses appeared as well as refinements of old courses — West African dressmaking, Mind that Child!, White City Mothers and Babies group, Indian dancing, A People's History of Islington, the Greenwich Free Minds Club, etc.

Community Groups

In trying to make the programmes of their centres more relevant to the interests and issues of the surrounding communities most outreach workers set up courses in conjunction with local organisations and amenity and action groups.

Some followed the models of the first welfare rights and planning courses and set up similar courses in conjunction with local citizens' rights and residents' action groups. Others set up courses on black studies or Asian studies in conjunction with local immigrant organisations. One outreach worker provided institute support for classes in the study of the Koran. At Addison we provided support for braille classes run by a self-help organisation of blind and partially sighted people called Projects By the Blind.

But not all the courses set up in conjunction with other organisations were necessarily to do with the specialised interests of the group concerned. Often outreach workers set up conventional adult education courses—dressmaking, keep-fit, arts and crafts—in conjunction with local groups, the only difference in the courses being that they were run on the group's own premises or that they formed part of the group's otherwise independently organised programme of activities. In 1973 a slim, business-like woman contacted Addison. She was the secretary of the women's league of a black community organisation. She was quite clear about the way we could help.

'Our numbers are down. We want a regular well-organised activity around which we can build up our other activities. We have a sewing circle that meets once a week. Can you provide us with a professional teacher and turn it into a proper dressmaking class?'

'If the institute supports your group,' I said, 'we would like to think that the class was open to anyone, black or white.'[25]

'Of course', the secretary said, then added after a pause. 'We are not a racist organisation.'

None of our regular tutors was available so I referred to the panel of tutors at County Hall. They supplied me with the name and address of a tutor living within a couple of streets of the church hall used by the women's league. I wrote to her, she replied, and I arranged to pick her up at her home and take her to meet the women's league committee. The woman who answered the door was in her middle thirties, charming-looking, quietly spoken... and black. I drove her to the church hall, my mind racing. What would the women's league think? Would they assume I had gone to a great deal of trouble to find them a black as opposed to a white tutor? Would they think that no white tutor had been willing to take the job on? Would they interpret my having provided them with one of the few black dressmaking tutors in the service as an act of condescending, 'do-gooding', unthinking but none the less blatant racism?

We arrived at the hall and the tutor met the women's league secretary and some of the committee. There was some slight trouble with accents at first since the tutor was Nigerian and all the other women were West Indian—would they think that I thought that being black was like being the same nationality? —but the encounter, an informal interview in fact, seemed to go reasonably well. I offered to drive the tutor home, but she said she would walk. As soon as she had left the secretary turned and looked at me. Her regard was not warm.

'How did you choose that woman?' she asked.

'She is on the panel of approved tutors. I got her name and address from County Hall.'

'Did you choose her because she was black?'

'No.'

She looked at me for a moment. 'She seems very suitable' she said.

Inter-agency Activities

Most outreach workers devoted a good part of their time to establishing relationships with statutory and voluntary agencies in their areas and involving their institutes in multi-agency activities. The agencies they worked with might include the local community relations council, the local voluntary services council, statutory social and welfare agencies, trades unions and local trades councils, housing trusts, the churches, neighbourhood councils, the probation service....

In 1976 Addison's outreach worker (replacing me while I was on leave) attended a meeting held by the Hammersmith Council for Community Relations at which one of their employment officers expressed concern at the low level of numeracy of many of his clients. He argued that formal courses were not the answer. Most of his clients needed only two or three sessions to remind them of skills they had learnt at school, or to overcome a block, or to bring their skill in one area, fractions say, up to the level required to pass a preliminary test in order to get a place on a government retraining scheme. The outreach worker approached the employment officer and together they decided to set up two 'maths surgeries' a week where people could drop in for advice and immediate tuition. They were given the use of a room by the local Employment Service Agency on Monday mornings and by the Hammersmith Resource Centre on Thursday afternoons. The local further education college provided the two tutors and shared the payment with Addison. Addison printed a leaflet and the two organisers circulated it through the Training Service Agency (who undertook to refer people who failed their tests), the job centres, the careers service, the youth service, social and community workers, the Citizens Advice Bureau and a borough advice centre.

The two sessions opened for business under the title of WIN (Walk-In-Numeracy) in November 1976 and by April 1977 were catering for up to twelve adults per meeting—as many as the tutors could handle. In 1977 the Training Service Agency took over the payment of the two tutors during the summer holiday period, and with their financial involvement the number of agencies that had provided funding, staffing, accommodation, or consistent administrative support had risen to six.

Non-course Activities
Through the establishment of these sorts of contact outreach workers often found themselves engaged in activities that bore little resemblance to formal courses. The outreach worker at Frobisher Institute lent his support to public meetings held by the Surrey Docks Action Group and worked with the Bowsprit Theatre Company to develop a theatrical programme on the issues raised by the Docklands Redevelopment Scheme. In North Kensington the outreach worker became a member of the advisory council of the Neighbourhood Law Centre, providing his support for much of the legal and community

action associated with the centre. Outreach workers found themselves helping run community festivals, street parties and book fairs, organising advice centres and using video in the streets. One helped establish an educational home visitors project and a luncheon club for young mothers. I offered Addison's help in revitalising the programme of a community hall and found myself working with three children on the first (and only) issue of a community newspaper for the two estates served by the hall. And another outreach worker found herself providing back-up for a group which proceeded to County Hall and confronted her own ultimate masters.

Image

As a natural adjunct to these activities outreach workers experimented with ways of advertising the institute's presence in the area, suggesting ways of improving the institute's publicity or making it more relevant, running information stalls, mounting exhibitions, dropping leaflets, giving talks, attending meetings, talking to individuals, seeking ways of encouraging demand and helping groups and individuals articulate those demands.

'It doesn't matter if it looks a little scruffy', the outreach worker from Kensington Institute said to me as we studied the design for a handout for a series of meetings called 'Out of Work?'. 'Better they identify us with the political guys handing out the leaflets than with the exchange.'

Out of Work?

'Out of Work?' was an attempt to provide support for people who were chronically unemployed. The outreach worker at Kensington Institute, a family man with children in their teens, had been unemployed himself two or three years earlier and it was his experience during that period — the gradual deterioration of spirit, the isolation — that had made him interested in setting up a series of meetings that might help others combat these and other horrors that accompany being out of work. I co-operated with him since the local employment exchange served the area covered by our two institutes. We talked the idea over between ourselves and with the manager of the local Employment Service Agency, and made approaches to other bodies in the area — the trades council, the local voluntary services council, and the Hammersmith Council for Community Relations. We enlisted the enthusiastic support of the HCCR employment officer and from that moment on he played an equal part in the organisation of the project. We did not decide on a pre-arranged list of topics for the meetings, but tried to anticipate the ways the meetings might go and sounded out a number of people — a member of a recently formed claimants' union, members of a local welfare rights group, an inspector with the Department of Health and Social Security — asking them to be available to come to a meeting if the group thought their presence might help. We also got together pamphlets and information on benefits and rights, further education and government retraining schemes. And perhaps most important of all, we asked friends who had experienced unemployment or were out of work at the time to come along if they could.

We decided to hold the meetings at Addison headquarters, about five minutes' walk from the employment exchange, on Tuesdays at 11 a.m., and for three weeks before the first meeting the HCCR employment officer, the Kensington outreach worker and I leafleted the main entrance to the exchange, talking to anyone interested in the idea. By the first meeting we had handed out more than 2,000 copies of a leaflet which said:

Out of work?
A chance to meet people sharing similar problems and to get information and help that could be useful.

The idea is to meet, pool information and, if you want to invite them, listen to speakers with specialist knowledge on rights, retraining, co-operative activities and community facilities.

The way the meetings go, the subjects discussed, are up to you.

Come along and see what you make of it.

We held six meetings during May and June 1975. Attendance varied between twelve and five, ending on eight. No clear programme was followed, but an enormous amount of

information was exchanged. Those that came talked, before
the meeting over coffee provided by the institute, during the
meeting, and in the street and pub afterwards. Some three or
four attended all the meetings. Others came for one meeting
only, and since we continued leafleting there was a small but
continual turnover. At the first meeting there was criticism of
the wording of the leaflet and the group rewrote it:

> *You are not the only one*
> We are a group of unemployed people.
>
> We meet together (for the moment) at the address
> overleaf on Tuesdays at 11.00 a.m. to talk about questions
> like:
> 1. If I am not entitled to unemployment benefit, how do
>   I get the money I need from social security?
> 2. Why should I work in a job I don't want?
> 3. How can I get the job I want?
> 4. How can I be retrained to get the job I want?
> 5. What is a claimants' union? (There is one starting up in
>   the area.)
> Come and join us.

By the fourth meeting the group decided that this wording
might discourage those suspicious of political action and for
the last two meetings we used a leaflet with much the same
wording as the first.

At the first meeting the HCCR employment officer, the
other outreach worker and I explained who we were and the
(limited) resources we could offer. We then asked the others if
they wanted to introduce themselves and the talking began.
One elderly man learnt that he could have a free pass on
public transport and one of the group undertook to arrange
this for him. A middle-aged black woman listened hard to
advice from another member of the group on where she could
get work as a machinist, and did not come back to the next
meeting. Others were interested in retraining schemes. We
distributed pamphlets and the HCCR employment officer
spoke on the subject and provided advice for individuals.
Someone asked about the Greater London Council's New
Town Scheme and I chased up information about it for the

next meeting. From the third meeting on, the inspector from the Department of Health and Social Security took to dropping in unofficially and helped demystify some of her department's practices and arranged for some of the members of the group to get benefits to which they were entitled. Some members admitted to despondency, depression and loneliness. One man realised, after a discussion of the way one should present oneself at a job-interview, that he had been selling himself short. Comments and criticisms were made of the way the local Employment Service Agency and Unemployment Benefits Department went about their work and these were passed back. At the fifth meeting one of the regulars said that the meetings had given him the confidence to admit that his 'spelling was bad', and that he had failed to get jobs in the past because he could not fill out application forms. I was able to refer him to Addison's literacy scheme and within a few days he was meeting a volunteer tutor and learning at last to read and write. At the last meeting an out-of-work builder and decorator, handicapped by chronic bronchitis, wheezed his way up to the Kensington outreach worker. He was holding a form and wanted the outreach worker to help him fill it out. This man was not illiterate. He was, like many of the literate public at large, confounded by the institute's own enrolment form. What he wanted to do was join one of Addision's art classes.[26]

Chapter 16

Experiment

Outreach work was by its nature almost entirely experimental, but it was not the only experimentation going on in adult education in the first half of the 1970s. Nor was all experimentation to do with community development and/or socio-political issues. Centres were experimenting with subject-matter, resulting in courses on water-divining, parapsychology, science fiction, rock music and cabaret. Attempts were being made to extend the subject, resulting in activities such as 'literacy through cookery'. Centres were rearranging their timetables to take into account people's working hours, resulting in classes related to shift hours in factories and courses with titles like 'Lunchtime Keep Fit for Businessmen'. A whole range of developments was taking place in the methods of teaching languages to leisure-motivated adults,[27] and at Central Wandsworth Institute in London, where the Allfarthing Family Workshop had been established, an extraordinary experiment was being conducted in the study of systems of wisdom.

New Philosophy Courses
In September 1974 Central Wandsworth Institute introduced four new courses into its programme and advertised them under the collective title 'New Philosophy'. The course descriptions hinted at a mood of yearning and search very different from the firmly ordinary feel of the standard adult education programme, and very different from the detached, analytical feel of many courses on philosophy in other sectors of the education service:

'Buddhism' is a course designed to show the beautiful tenets of the Buddhist view of the world. The starting point at each meeting will be the experience of meditation.

'Astrology' will deal with the setting up of birth charts and the position and meanings of the planets. Through this astrology reveals itself as an ancient and wise system capable of generating immensely valuable insights into our own life.

'Chinese philosophy—I Ching studies'. Three thousand years ago the Chinese were using a book of oracles to guide their decisions. Through the ages the Book of Changes (I Ching) has developed into a work of great wisdom . . .

'Mandala' literally means circle . . . . It is perhaps the oldest and most pervasive of all symbols which might be said to express the wholeness of the world within us and the world without . . .

The organiser of the courses, a full-time member of the institute's staff, expressed his aims in these terms: 'I wanted to organise something beyond the normal liberal studies programme. I matured in the sixties when there was a re-awakening of interest in the esoteric arts and a reaction against intellectualism. These courses seemed the natural thing for me to do. Without realising it at first I found myself expressing my age and milieu.'

The organiser had prepared the ground for the courses by reading widely, talking to a wide range of people, making contact with various organisations, and choosing his tutors carefully, 'looking for people with exceptional gifts, wise men and women'. He and his tutors had gone carefully over possible developments in each course and in the courses as a group. They had discussed the kinds of student the courses might attract, how individuals and groups might react, how to overcome people's diffidence towards 'philosophy' and 'mysticism', how to stress in publicity and prove in practice that qualifications were unnecessary and that approaching these subjects without any prior knowledge of them could even prove an advantage.

The response to the publicity was good and each course was fully enrolled. The people in all four groups came largely from the locality of the institute and included men and women from different age groups and different social and professional backgrounds. And the courses worked, each developing a life of its own, a group identity and a sense of communal search—a 'glow', as the organiser described it.

During that first year a residential weekend was held to which people from all four courses went in order to meet, listen to lectures and discuss some of the apparent paradoxes thrown up by the comparison of these differing approaches to insight. The weekend proved so useful that in the following year, in order to increase the opportunities for this pooling of knowledge, two residential weekends were held and a series of lectures introduced at the institute, drawing on the subject-matter and experience of all the 'new philosophy' courses and beyond. In this year also, a second stage in astrology was added and a course on mythology. The mood of the 'new philosophy' group of courses is expressed even more clearly in the description of the mythology course:

> Myths, like many sciences and arts of the past, are gaining a finer appreciation. The attempt to decipher the myths and symbols of our ancient forebears leads beyond a lesson in history to the enrichment of our own consciousness. The worlds described by myth are strange and mysterious but they have a resonance in our own perceptions of reality that is powerful and vital . . . .

The lecture series became established, drawing on tutors of existing courses and visitors, and covering such subjects as:

William Blake—a new kind of man
Modern science and meditation
Dreams, symbols and extra-sensory perception
Western traditions in symbolism—the Qabalah; the Tarot
Symbol and myth in Tantric Buddhism
Another kind of space
Consciousness
Symbol in art

But 'lecture' is not quite the word. The last three subjects, for example, were meetings in which a group of thirty to forty people were arranged in tiers of chairs, some set on tables, around an artist and his spotlit canvas. For a total of seven or eight hours the artist, who was also a student in the Chinese philosophy class, painted and conversed with the group about his concept of the way painting had developed, his search for a release from perspective into abstract symbolism and another kind of space, and the way in which his involvement in the 'new philosophy' programme had affected him and his painting. By 1976 the lecture series was established and proving a testing-ground for new additions to the programme. The 1976-7 programme consisted of courses on 'Fundamentals of Astrology', 'Further Explorations in Astrology', 'Buddhist Meditation and Philosophy', 'Chinese Philosophy—I Ching Studies', 'Mythology', the Open Lecture Series on 'Myth, Dream and Symbol' and a course on 'Dreams and Dreaming'. But it is easy to list subjects. What is difficult to convey is the excitement and enthusiasm generated by the programme, the atmosphere of complete and open-minded exchange, the talking till dawn at the residential weekends and till midnight under the street lamp outside the institute branch, the sense of being on the track of something very important and in the company of others.

The organiser[28] is happy to acknowledge that he started the experiment. 'But then it flowered', he said. 'It happened on its own. I stand on the sidelines and am awed and amazed.'

Chapter 17

Two Outside Influences

Experiment and outreach work developed from within the adult education service as an expression of its already existing character. Two further developments, this time imposed on adult education from outside, helped reinforce the shift to a wider community involvement. The first of these was the launching of a nationwide campaign to combat adult illiteracy.

Literacy

Nothing indicates more clearly how adult education had lost any direct connection with its past than the state of its literacy provision. During the nineteenth century a considerable part of adult education consisted of men and women gathering together to learn to read and write, but in the 1950s and 1960s adult education's role as provider of literacy classes for adults had almost disappeared. Many centres would have a few token classes in general education, but as late as 1970 you could find classes in which—under the supervision of a single tutor—there were immigrants learning English as a second language, some literate and some illiterate in their mother tongues; immigrants trying to come to grips with a dialect of English very different from their own; English men and women in varying stages of literacy; somebody wanting to learn how to write reports and somebody else trying to catch up on 'maths'. The poverty of this provision can only be explained by the fact that literacy and numeracy classes were so alien to the rest of the adult education programme, so out of place, that adult educators had put them last on their list of priorities or simply forgotten about them altogether.

What little serious adult literacy provision there was in the country at the end of the 1960s was supplied by independent and voluntary agencies such as the settlements. Cambridge House, a settlement and social action centre in south-east London, is an example. In the mid 1960s it started its literacy project, matching adults with reading and writing difficulties on a one-to-one basis with volunteer tutors. The scheme started with only a handful of clients but grew until, in 1973, the settlement had something like 500 clients on its books — and a grim idea of just how many other people there were for whom it was unable to cater. This experience had been repeated by other settlements providing literacy tuition, and in 1973 the British Association of Settlements began a campaign to alert people to the size of the problem of adult illiteracy and to press for government action. BAS held a conference and put out a pamphlet entitled *A Right to Read* in which it estimated that more than two million adults in the country had a reading age of less than nine years.

In 1974 the BBC began drawing up plans for a TV programme to go out three times a week, one of those a peak viewing time, aimed at motivating adults with reading and writing problems to seek help, and informing them of where that help could be found. Discussions were held at government level, with BAS and with education authorities, and a pilot programme was designed. The BBC undertook to broadcast a phone number at the end of each programme and to refer all enquiries to the relevant authority, and the government undertook to set up an agency to inject funds into the scheme in order to help the various agencies cater for the referrals. With the BBC moving and the government helping, only one small problem remained. Who was actually going to teach all these newly motivated adults to read and write once they had been fired by the nationwide campaign? The answer in almost every case was adult education.

Local education authorities instructed their adult education services to tool up, to increase the number of general education classes, to redirect their resources, to rethink their priorities, find more part-time tutors in literacy skills and begin training volunteers to teach adult illiterates on a one-to-one basis. Few authorities made more funds available. All they asked was that a service, which for some years now had been concerned with the provision of leisure learning only, should rearrange its priorities and in less than a year commit a significant amount of its time, energies and resources to an area of learning largely alien to its prevailing philosophy.

But reorganisation and reallocation were part of the everyday administrative experience in adult education. Adult education was also experienced in the training of part-time tutors, and in the business of recruiting them and often introducing them to teaching for the first time. And adult education was the one sector of the education service used to dealing with adult students of a variety of levels of knowledge or skill and from a variety of backgrounds; and experienced in responding to students' genuinely personal requirements. The poor cousin, in short, was no newcomer to the business of making do under pressure and with few resources.

Limited funds — £1 million for the whole country during the first year — were made available through the Adult Literacy Resource Agency, although initially to help local projects get under way rather than sustain them. The agency began calling for applications for funds and dispensing them early in 1975; and the effect of these small but readily available disbursements was to jog half-interested authorities and agencies into action.

The first BBC programme, called 'On the Move', went out in October 1975 and adult education centres round the country began taking and for the most part competently catering for the brunt of the referrals.

This literacy work still remains a small part of a largely leisure learning provision, but its influence on adult education has been enormous. Until 1974 the experimentation in adult education, the changes in thinking and approach, had been taking place in pockets of the country. The literacy campaign was nationwide, forcing even the most reluctant adult educators to respond if only because they were receiving referrals from the BBC. It forced adult educators to rethink their priorities, take a hard look at the way they were currently making use of their resources, experiment with their programmes and exploit their flexibility. The adult education service as a whole was forced to recognise that the provision of of a very different kind of learning was indeed a valid part of its role.

Financial Cuts

And then came the financial cuts. 1974 saw them introduced and 1975 saw them bite. The British economy was on a downhill slide and inflation was beginning to gallop; and education like everything else was being minutely studied at both government and local authority level in a search for ways of cutting public expenditure. Adult education found itself being cut in many authorities or at best being put on a no-growth basis, which with inflation meant in reality being cut.

Even to contemplate cutting a sector of the education service that accounted for less than 2 per cent of the national education budget may seem small-minded — grotesque, in fact, when one considers that it is the sector best able to provide learning situations on demand, and to help some of those thrown into unemployment to deal with their new-found 'leisure' in a personally valuable way.

But the cuts did put adult educators on their toes and had them casting round for convincing arguments to justify their existence. And since hobbies and interests were unlikely to carry much weight in the council chambers across the country, even those adult educators who had been most resistant to these recent developments began pointing to adult education's role as a supporting service to community development, and to adult education's work with the disadvantaged. How, they shouted at local level, through their professional associations and even by lobbying Parliament, could anyone contemplate cutting back something that rendered such valuable service to the handicapped, the housebound mother, the old-age pensioner, the immigrant, the socially disadvantaged, the shy and the illiterate? Community involvement suddenly became the ticket to survival, and those whose protestations rang a little hollow because they were unable to back them up with facts quickly set about putting matters right.

The cuts were unwelcome but they did play a part in consolidating the changes in the first half of the 1970s. They were the final nudge that set the community bandwagon on the road.

PART IV
Survival Learning

Chapter 18

Leisure Learning and Survival Learning

The changes in the service in the first half of the 1970s demonstrated that adult education could provide two very different kinds of learning experience: *leisure learning,* which is to do with the extras in people's lives, their hobbies and interests, their quiet desires; and *survival learning,* which is to do with the essentials in people's lives, rights, housing, learning to read and write, learning the language of one's adopted country, people's pressing needs.

Of course there are pitfalls in such distinctions. The adult educator might be tempted to choose between them and, spurred on by his social conscience, plump for the second as more significant and more deserving of his energies than the first. But the last thing I want to do is suggest that adult education should give itself over entirely to the provision of, survival learning. The basic character of adult education is to be found in the apparently non-controversial provision of leisure learning, and it is there that the particular strengths and qualities of adult education are continually and quietly restated. Having the broad provision of leisure learning as a base makes experiment in the provision of survival learning possible.

Nor does the identification of the two types of learning experience suggest that they are therefore mutually exclusive. Both elements can occur in the same activity, and the extent to which the experience is one of leisure or survival learning will depend as much on the individual student's circumstances and motives for attending as it will on the style and subject-matter of the activity itself. A woman may attend a dressmaking class as a practical way of filling a spare evening each week. Another may attend because she cannot afford to dress herself and her family any other way. And in one dressmaking class, in an affluent suburb of an affluent city in Australia, a middle-class woman once said with sudden earnestness: 'I came here because I wanted to learn to do something. Because I felt so inadequate.'

Dignity

The word 'survival' is a strong one and deliberately chosen. There may be times when adult education can provide learning experiences that will actually contribute to an individual's physical survival — a course that informs the elderly (or those in contact with the elderly) of benefits available could certainly provide heating and food for someone in the dead of winter who might otherwise be missed by the hard-pressed social services. But these literally life-or-death cases must be rare. What adult education can and often does provide are learning experiences that enable people to regain a sense of personal dignity. And to survive as a complete human being, a sense of dignity can be just as important as food and warmth. The woman in the dressmaking class in Eastwood Evening College in Sydney sought a sense of personal dignity through the acquisition of a skill. A group of people learning about their rights want to play an active, knowledgeable role in their own lives rather than be cravenly at the mercy of the agency that doles out assistance. And the man in the 'Out of Work?' group, just a hair's breadth from being a dosser, said it this way: 'This is the first time I ever told anyone I had trouble reading and writing. This group's given me hope.'

Political Education

This distinction between leisure and survival learning may show up in the differing reasons people have for attending the same course, but it is also to be found in the style and objectives of the courses themselves. There *are* obvious differences between 'Masters of Modern Painting' and the course

called 'Out of Work?'. And once the adult educator actively
engages in the provision of a course like 'Out of Work?' or
welfare rights, or literacy, or housing, he must face up to the
realities of life He must realise that while leisure learning is
educational, survival learning is educational *and* political.[29]

As long as adult education concerned itself with the provision of leisure learning alone, all was quiet and uncomplicated. Provision for the working class meant providing instruction
and support for so-called working-class pursuits. ('Where,'
lamented a member of the old guard at a conference in 1974
amidst a debate introduced by one of the new guard on adult
education's role in the class struggle, 'have all the pigeon-
fancying classes gone?') Provision for the elderly meant running
a singing club for the over-sixties and for the physically
handicapped a music and movement class. Hobbies, pastimes
and time-fillers were provided either unilaterally by the centre
itself or at the request of some recognised and statutorily
approved body such as the local welfare department or the
Red Cross. And when adult education did dabble in current
issues such as race it would adopt the form of a series of
lectures by accredited experts under some antiseptic title such as
'Race Relations in Britain Today' or run it under the aegis of
an extramural department of a university using an academic
as the tutor and calling it 'The Sociology of Race'.

But survival learning is harder than that, more real, grittier,
gutsier. It is to do with knowledge versus ignorance, power
rather than powerlessness, equipping people to represent
themselves, providing them with the skills necessary to affect
their own condition, so that they can decide where they want
to go and how to get there.

Survival learning does not replace leisure learning as a
major contribution of adult education nor negate the validity
of any activity that is largely leisure learning in content.
Rather, survival learning complements leisure learning,
adding to the character of an activity and rounding out a
centre's overall provision, making it more relevant to the
affairs and issues within the community. The over-sixty singing
club stays, but the centre also investigates the potential
demand for a course on pensioners' rights. The formal course
on race relations stays, but the centre looks for ways of
responding to the requirements of immigrant groups in the

area, perhaps in the form of language classes or meetings on the techniques of community self-help or by providing a course that lets black people tell it how it is. Or perhaps planning has become a red-hot issue as it did in Clapham, with plans being drawn up, public meetings held and large-scale redevelopment under way. Some people are desperate to keep the place unchanged, others are only too glad to see the bulldozers move in but worried about compensation or whether they will have any say in where they will be rehoused. Some of these people are looking for information quickly. One of them attends a woodcarving class at the local adult education centre, and now approaches the head of the centre to see if the centre can help . . . .

Chapter 19

Listening and Learning

The move towards a more realistic involvement in the community requires a new humility on the part of the adult educator. He must adopt techniques that are the antithesis of the set-'em-up-and-see method of programme design. He must train himself to listen and learn.

The White City Estate

The White City estate is large and ugly. It houses about 6,000 people and is made up of thirty massive, five-storey brick boxes set in bleak rows round a large square of flat ground and low amenity buildings. The north side is bordered by Western Avenue with commercial traffic racing down off the elevated Westway twenty-four hours a day. The eastern border consists of White City stadium. The southern side is marked off by a heavy-duty steel fence and Queen's Park Rangers football ground. And down the western side runs Bloemfontein Road in a straight line from the impersonal roar of Western Avenue, past the estate, then through an area of nineteenth-century housing until it reaches scruffy, friendly Shepherd's Bush.

The estate is equipped with two churches, a church primary school, a youth club, a one o'clock club, where parents can bring babies and toddlers over the middle of the day, an adventure playground, two ILEA infants' schools and an ILEA junior school. There are two pubs, one on the estate and another through the steel fence next to the football ground. Across Bloemfontein Road is a park with a swimming pool, and Christopher Wren and Hammersmith County comprehensive schools, which in the evenings become a branch of

Addison Institute. On balance, on paper, you could say that the estate was not badly supplied with some of the necessary community services. But there is also an overpowering sense of twentieth-century squalor. The flats are low-ceilinged, and reached by climbing blank stairways and walking along exposed cement walk-ways. The drab, oversize architecture and the layout remove the place in atmosphere and character from the rest of the Shepherd's Bush and Hammersmith area. That central square is ugly. There is no bus in Bloemfontein Road and very few shops. Problems have a habit of multiplying. When the caretakers employed by the Greater London Council went on strike, the dustmen employed by the local borough observed the picket line, adding the problem of piles of refuse to the problems of lack of supervision and maintenance. And although this is vociferously denied by the GLC some of the tenants allege that the estate is being used by the GLC to house their problem families, that in other words it has become a dumping estate.

The amenities, given a second glance, do not always come up to scratch. The adventure playground is set on the unrelieved ground of the central square — no sense of a park, or the intimacy of a scruffy back yard here. The youth club is battered, part boarded up, dark and dingy (and at the time of writing, closed). The one o'clock club has a play area that is wind-blasted in winter and treeless in summer. And the adult education provision in that branch of Addison Institute just over the road is minimal.

Addison has the use of a large complex of modern school buildings, but by 1974 was running little else there except activities that could make use of the two schools' specialised craft rooms and gymnasia. Who was to blame for the downward spiral? Had the institute cut back its programme because people did not come, or did people not come because the institute offered such a limited programme? There was a beginners' French class there. But the French tutor said that hers was the only occupied room in a whole wing and once the night closed in, apart from the occasional howls and shrieks from the gyms, she and her class had the impression that they were the only souls left in the world. The class, which dropped in numbers rapidly, left the building in a bunch at nine, and the women demanded a male escort along Bloemfontein Road. The class was closed at the end of the year and the tutor given work at another branch. One more loop down the spiral.

The Mothers and Babies Club

It was with Addison's provision in the area in this moribund state and a growing sense on the part of the institute's full-time staff that something should be done that a group worker attached to a settlement approached Addison and asked for help. There was a room upstairs in the youth club which with a bit of cleaning out might do for a mothers and babies club — the mothers meeting and talking with the babies crawling about and playing. She had a list of women who might be interested and had scheduled meetings for early Monday afternoons. Could the institute design a programme of talks and provide the speakers?

Yes, of course. If the people from the estate did not want to cross Bloemfontein Road to the institute, then we would have to go to them, and here was a perfect opportunity to do just that. I enthusiastically set about planning a series of ten meetings, some on music and crafts, and some on subjects that I and the group worker thought would be relevant to the women, such as infant education and home management.

But the White City Mothers and Babies Club did not last the distance. Within six weeks it had ceased to exist.

After a preliminary meeting with some of the women we held the first of the ten proposed meetings, to which I invited a speaker who played tapes and talked about musical comedy. On the second Monday the same speaker came again and this time played tapes of English folk music and taught the group two folk dances. These two meetings were fun. Eight women came. The babies crawled underfoot or at the end of the room during the dancing. Tea was made and there was a lot of uninhibited, friendly chat.

On the third Monday I brought along Addison's video kit. Addison's media resources officer showed the group how to operate the kit and then, operating it themselves, the women made a tape about their club. I was charged with showing the tape at the one o'clock club on the estate later in the week, which I did.

A reasonable, though smaller number of women gathered for the fourth meeting expecting another session of folk dancing but the speaker did not turn up. Or rather, he did but found the door of the youth club closed. Such was the dismal, lifeless look of the building, with its wired windows, cracked panes and scratched and scrawled-upon paintwork, that after waiting a few minutes on the pavement outside and discerning no movement behind the upstairs windows where the group was patiently waiting, the speaker departed. Left to their own devices, the women chatted in a desultory fashion and the group broke up early.

Two more meetings took place. I sent letters to all those who had attended or shown any interest in the club. Three turned up to hear an infants' school headmistress talk on child development. And no one from the estate turned up to hear a woman journalist talk on womens' rights.

That is not to say that the journalist did not have an audience. The meeting took place, but it was like a scene from a crudely satirical play about community workers. The journalist spoke for an hour with a group composed of two community workers from the settlement, me, a woman connected with the administration of the youth club and a woman who had moved away from White City four weeks earlier and had come back for a visit. No one told the journalist that none of us actually lived on the estate.

Demand Versus Need

The group worker was put out by the rapid demise of the mothers and babies club. She and the health visitor who had furnished the original list of women had been sure that there was a *need* for the kind of activity we had tried to provide.

But this concept of 'need' is a slippery one. Professionals in the community industry are forever talking about identifying and meeting needs. This means getting out there in the community, deciding what is lacking—a health clinic, community spirit, somewhere for the teenagers to let off steam, happiness—and then trying to fill the gap. But identifying needs can easily imply condescension. The outside agency, the 'expert', is brought in or comes in uninvited to discern and then inform the needy of what they lack. The possibility of the needy being able to speak up for themselves may not always be considered. There may even be the assumption that the needy may not know that they are in need unless they are told. This can easily lead to the idea that the agency knows best, to a disguised authoritarianism, and to the application of subtle pressure to make the needy acquiesce in a provision 'that will be good for them'. There are even times when it is difficult not to suspect that certain needs have been identified because the agency undertaking the research has a vested interest in identifying the needs in the first place. Thus teenagers who want jobs and the cash that goes with them end up with an adventure playground instead.

In the case of the White City mothers and babies club the group worker came in from outside and 'identified the need' for the club. Since she bore the title 'group worker' it is not too surprising that she identified the need for a group. I was then called in and, after the most perfunctory consultation with some of the women involved, arranged a series of meetings that *I* felt would be appropriate for *them*. And to complete this text-book case of manipulation the group itself was recruited with the help of a health visitor, who suggested to some of the women that they should attend.

To avoid these sorts of pitfalls, the adult educator must concern himself with demands rather than needs. This is not to say that he can sit back and wait for people to come to him. Some demands may be expressed in neat, articulate, unambiguous forms but others will lie deep within a situation or series of events, only to be formulated and expressed after investigation, questioning and repeated consultation and discussion. The adult educator must research his community as thoroughly as any community worker bent upon identifying needs, but he must set out to listen and learn. He must come to a community or situation with as few preconceived notions as possible. His aims should be to locate and respond as far as he is able to people's demands when they are clearly expressed; and to help people formulate and articulate their demands when the demands are not clearly expressed.

The distinction between need and demand is important for the adult educator engaged in community education, since one can begin with the best intention of learning from those it is one's job to work with, but very quickly end up imposing one's own ideas on them. It is like working with some chemically unstable substance. The educationally valid business of enabling people to help themselves can dissolve all too rapidly into social engineering by an outside agency.[30]

Blurred Objectives

There had been two objectives in my mind when I organised such an unconnected collection of subjects and activities for the mothers and babies club. I had wanted to try a variety of ideas until one clicked, then build a course on that. It may have been a blunt-edged way of doing it but at least my heart was in the right place. But my other objective was more suspect. My hope was that the ten meetings would be a success; that the news that they were both entertaining and useful would spread; and that the group would grow until we were obliged to open up other activities on other days in that room at the youth club — a keep-fit group, perhaps, or an arts and crafts class. I had even hoped that after a couple of years, having demonstrated our usefulness and having won the interest of a sufficient number of people on the estate, we might be able to coax some of them into joining some of the evening activities in the schools over the road. Rather than organise a course that would be of benefit to the women who attended, I was trying to convert them into agents who would infiltrate the estate, putting the case for adult education.

If I had genuinely attended to the demands of that group we would have had the speaker on music for the whole ten weeks. He was first-rate and the group sensed it immediately. Ten weeks with him and they would have acquired or extended their appreciation of a surprising number of forms of music. They would also, incidentally, have had demonstrated very effectively what adult education was about and what it could do. But instead, on the third week, I brought along the video kit.

Ironically the tape itself was good, and my principal asked me to show it to an inspector to demonstrate the sort of work we were doing on the estate. I remember watching the tape with the principal and inspector in the principal's office, hearing the woman who had taken on the task of interviewing the rest of the group express her gratitude to Addison Institute and hearing my own voice prompting another woman towards the end of the tape into saying that anyone was welcome to join the group and ask for talks on the subjects they wanted. The tape rolled to its cloying end and the principal, the inspector and I sat about briefly, smiling with satisfaction at one another. Evidence captured with the use of a modern electronic device of Addison doing good work down among the disadvantaged.

Then, of course, the speaker on music could not get in and the mothers and babies club was on the road to extinction. It was at this point that I should have realised that something was very wrong. Left without a speaker the women had nothing particular to talk about or do. There was no substance to their meeting. But this was the fourth week. If the women had actually been learning something, then by the fourth meeting they would already have had fuel enough to continue by themselves. One of the features of a good adult education course is that when the tutor falls ill at the last moment or finds himself twiddling his thumbs in a train that has been held up between stations for half an hour, the class, being adults gathered together for a purpose, can usually get on usefully with the business of the meeting themselves. But nothing like this happened with the mothers and babies club. The hotchpotch that I had served up for them was not educational. My objectives had been wrong.

Wrap-up
But the women stopped coming.

Having no one turn up concentrates the adult educator's mind wonderfully. During the last dismal meeting of the mothers and babies club I began to understand why we had gone wrong, and why from the third meeting on I had found the whole thing such a bind. I was vastly relieved when the aggrieved and disappointed group worker agreed to call it a day. We sent out a letter to everyone who had ever attended, couched in language that hid her disappointment and my relief, saying that for the moment there would be no further meetings. The reason given was the approaching summer. We made no mention of the fact that in the simplest possible way every single one of them had indicated that what we were providing was not what they wanted, and that they were not going to be manipulated. In a perverse, negative, paradoxical way the result was a victory.[31]

Chapter 20

Educational Objectives

If the programme provided for the White City mothers and
babies club was not educational, what then was missing? What
are the elements necessary to make an adult education activity
genuinely educational and not something else — training,
entertainment, expert advice — that could be better provided
by some other agency?

Productive Social Contact
Adult education is a co-operative activity and this social aspect
is one of its most important features. Few activities will really
succeed if they do not contain opportunities for social contact.
The time-honoured tea-break plays its part, but social contact
should be fostered in the classroom as well. Often this comes
about naturally as a result of the relaxed atmosphere of
adult education activities, particularly in the crafts and physical activity classes. But a language or liberal studies class can
fail miserably despite excellent presentation of material if each
student remains an isolated unit facing the front and only
entering into a one-to-one relationship with the tutor.

This may go some way to explaining why film appreciation
classes often fail to generate an atmosphere of genuine search,
and quickly dwindle in numbers. The film course may seem
exciting in prospect, but for much of the time each student is
an isolated unit staring at the screen and not even entering into
a relationship with the tutor.

Ostensibly the White City mothers and babies club was
formed to combat isolation on the estate and foster social
contact. But the group worker and I failed to provide a

continuing co-operative activity that would have given the social contact meaning. What social contact there was was not *productive*, with the result that when that original member returned to the sixth meeting to say hello not one of the other women from the estate was there.

Learning

An adult education activity should involve learning. This may seem so obvious as to be not worth saying, but in fact many adult education centres find themselves supporting activities from which learning has largely disappeared. Dressmaking is an example. Many of these classes are run without an ordered syllabus. Each class member simply gets on with her particular dress or blouse or jacket or skirt and the tutor advises each individual in turn. What can happen in such a case is that the class becomes consolidated into a permanent group of people who come together year after year, not to learn any new tricks but simply to make their own clothes in the company of each other and with the use of the centre's machines. The dress-making class becomes a sewing circle.

But dressmaking is an easy target. Porcelain restoration is a subject that involves a number of disciplines and requires great application. The student must master a set of intricate manual skills, he must understand the methods used to make the original pieces, he must learn to appreciate the artistic merit of the porcelain he is working with, and gain a knowledge of the traditions from which the damaged pieces come. Addison runs several classes in this subject. The tutor is second to none and people flock to hear his lectures and work under his supervision. It would be difficult to find a set of courses in which more learning took place . . . . And yet one or two people in the advanced class who attended year after year seemed to work apart, bringing in a damaged piece of china, then a porcelain figure, then a large chipped bowl, repairing each piece expertly and only seeking an occasional word of advice from the tutor on the particularly tricky bits. The impression finally gained was of a production line. They were buying up damaged pieces, repairing them in class, and selling them off afterwards at a profit. Not that there is anything intrinsically wrong with that. That a student studies a subject with the

object of profiting from his knowledge, financially or otherwise, is what education is about. But were they still learning?

Self-discovery
With not much learning going on, the White City mothers and
babies club offered precious little scope for self-discovery. Yet
the encouragement of self-discovery should be central to any
adult education activity. Adults have a wealth of knowledge
gained simply from living as independent human beings. Part
of adult education's role is to make the student aware of his
latent knowledge and skills. Part of the delight of adult
learning is the rediscovery of things already known, the
realisation that one is already part way there. A tutor made a
breakthrough with an illiterate adult when he learnt that the
student had worked for some years in a greengrocer's. The
tutor asked the student to draw the price flags to be stuck in
the stacks of vegetables. The student discovered he already had
a knowledge of the written language to build on.

At the City Literary Institute in London a style of teaching
music theory has been developed that is particularly suitable
for adults. The assumption is that although the student may be
musically illiterate he nevertheless 'knows how music works' as
a result of years of listening to, hearing, whistling, humming
or singing music in the ordinary course of his life. In the first
lesson the tutor teaches the class two simple figures used to
write music, explains what they represent and then plays a very
short musical phrase that cries out to be finished. Students
automatically hum the end and the tutor hands out manu-
script with the phrase he has played written on it and asks the
students to record their endings. He then collects in the
manuscripts, sits down at the piano and plays his students'
compositions. The point is made. Within an hour each student
has been able to compose, and write down, a bar of music.
The long haul ahead does not appear so formidable now that
the student realises that he has already covered part of the
ground.

Self-esteem
Once having made a person aware of his abilities the adult
educator is well on his way to achieving the underlying aim of

all adult education activities—that of raising the student's self-esteem. That music student will feel a sense of achievement in having composed a bar of music. An already very skilled pottery student will feel a sense of pride in refining his skills and producing an even better pot. If genuine learning is taking place, then step by step the participants will feel themselves growing as human beings.

The phrase 'raising the student's self-esteem' may sound rather grandiose, but adult education can be very realistic about its goals, and self-esteem should be interpreted just as realistically. A person who cannot read or write cannot laugh over Andy Capp. He cannot add his contribution to the graffiti on the poster advertising the film *Sweet and Sexy*. He cannot join his friends in the betting shop because he cannot read the racing form. All ordinary enough activities which you and I can take or leave, but an illiterate adult has to leave. Learning to read and write will enable him to gain access to these and a myriad other activities. And being able to do them, being able to take them or leave them, will raise his self-esteem.

Individual Change
'Self-discovery' and 'self-esteem' may also sound too self-centred, but that is all to the good if it helps stress that adult education has nothing to do with the doctrine, apparently still widely held in other sectors of the education service, and even perhaps gaining ground, of preparing the student or pupil to take his or her place in society, of preparing the pupil or student to play a specific role in the country's economy, that is of moulding the cogs or, as a head-teacher I once had the gothic experience of teaching under expressed it at a prize-giving ceremony, 'training future ratepayers'.

The danger is that when adult education veers towards community work it can fall into the same trap, not of course of training future ratepayers, but of keeping current ratepayers quiescent. That is what the mothers and babies club was doing—providing distraction for the moment without providing an opportunity for those involved to consider why they were judged to be in need of this special treatment. The meetings were simply filling in the odd Monday afternoon (and evidently not doing that very well either). They were helping the women mark time rather than move towards some sort of change.

One can sum up the elements described above — productive social contact, learning, self-discovery, raising the student's self-esteem — by saying that adult education should effect change. But brainwashing and indoctrination effect change too, so it is necessary to add that change in the adult education context should involve not only the change itself but making the student aware of his own potential for change and his potential for effecting further change himself. As a student learns a little about music he should also become aware that he can, if he wants, learn more and the methods by which he can do it. Brainwashing dulls, and indoctrination defines and limits one's perceptions of the world; but an educational experience, in no matter how specialised or how general a subject, should open up the mind.

Chapter 21

The Bingo Red Herring

The Question

'But what', comes the worried question, 'if they ask for bingo?' What indeed if I had successfully got across to the White City mothers and babies club the idea that I was there to respond to their demands and the women had promptly asked for a regular session of bingo?

Well, there is no reason automatically to draw the line at bingo. It is certainly possible for bingo to form a part, even a pivotal part, of some larger activity that is clearly educational; as in the case of a self-help project conducted by the elderly and involving courses on pensioners' rights, meetings on management skills, and the redesigning of a community centre's programme to include a bingo session run by themselves. It does seem unlikely, however, that a bingo session set up for no purpose other than playing bingo would be genuinely educational. In my experience at least, bingo does not effect change. It involves little or no learning; offers little or no opportunity for self-discovery; is unlikely to raise the individual's self-esteem; and does not even offer much scope for productive social contact.

Even so, adult educators should never automatically turn away from such a request. When they involve themselves in their community they should exchange information and wherever feasible co-operate with all the other agencies in the area, working their adult education programme into the whole pattern of community services available.[32] In this case they might pass the request for bingo on to the county or borough social services or recreation department, or to a community worker, or to the local representatives of the entertainments industry. And even then they must stay in touch in case the next request from the same quarter should prove to be for something that does fall within their brief.

The Underlying Anxiety

But bingo is well supplied by the entertainments industry and a demand for it is unlikely. When adult educators talk about bingo they are often expressing the anxiety that once they accept that adult education has a duty to respond to community demand, they will become ciphers; that somehow, overnight, from being the boss, the one who decides what goes into a centre's programme and what does not, they will become someone who is at the beck and call of any and everyone in the community.

There are two answers to this. The first is that only rarely will fifteen or twenty people march into the centre and demand a course. Community demand is normally expressed in much less direct ways—through suggestions from the other community agencies, through consultative committees of one sort or another, through requests from individuals, in casual conversations with students and people from the area, through the attendance statistics, through outside activities and events. For the most part adult educators will go on as before, having to take the initiative themselves in the design of their programmes. Indeed, what I am advocating is not a radical change in the centre's structure or even its programme, but an adjustment in the adult educator's philosophy and a realistic recognition of the basic forces at work in adult education.

The other answer is that adult educators are not under an obligation to respond willy-nilly to *any* demand. Their concern is to formulate an *educational* response to *community* demand. But to do this they must know what is and what is not educational in a community situation. In deciding how many badminton classes to include in their programme this year and what sort of commitment they should make to the campaign to combat illiteracy, in deciding whether they should increase the number of yoga classes or respond to a request for a course on the politics of black power, they must endeavour to strike a balance between what they feel are genuine community demands and what they see as genuinely educational.

That is not the job of a cipher.

Chapter 22

Standards

Adult education need not be academic. An adult education activity need not imitate the pedagogic style, the abstraction of knowledge, the division of knowledge into disciplines, or the denial of emotional, personal and political involvement that are sometimes part of the academic approach.

Race Relations

In 1971 as part of its special studies programme Addison ran a course called 'Race Relations'. The course was a series of formal lectures on a number of pre-arranged subjects given by academics or people working for research agencies in the field of race relations. Each week a group of white adults would gather and listen gravely to a lecture on 'Immigration and schooling — the Language Factor' or 'The Development of the Educational System of Modern India' or 'The West Indian Immigrant' or 'What can we Learn from Holland?' On one occasion a research psychologist spoke at some length on the ease or difficulty with which young children in one of the home counties could tell the difference between black and white dolls; and that particular evening was no more relevant to the institute's area or to the vital and emotionally charged subject of race than the activities going on in the ceramic repair class on the floor above.

But at one meeting in that series a local minister of religion came as the guest speaker. He was black and what he had to say was related to local conditions and grew out of his own experience. He came to argue a case, and he had notified the local press that he would be speaking, indicating that he saw his talk not so much as part of an adult education course but as another opportunity to continue his campaign for a more equitable treatment of the black immigrant population. And it was just this commitment, this personal and emotional involvement, that made the evening valuable.

Black Experience
Having taken the point, Addison ran another course on the subject of race in the following year. But this time the course was called 'Black Experience', and all the speakers were black.

The course co-ordinator was West Indian, an erudite man with a wealth of contacts in the black community in London, a lecturer and writer, and an occasional director of West Indian theatre and dance. He was also no mean bongo player. He was described by the officer at the Community Relations Commission who recommended him as a 'black man's black' and this he certainly was if by that one means a person uncompromisingly critical of the Europeans' past and present exploitation of the black races, and a passionate advocate of the recognition of the culture that has grown in the Caribbean as a result of the meeting there of African, Asian, European and other racial and cultural influences. But he was not a man so consumed by his black anger that he would not talk to whites. On the contrary, his life seemed entirely given over to arguing the case for the recognition of a West Indian black identity to any and all comers, and he had developed a wonderful way of chuckling incredulously when dealing with the more horrific details of West Indian history so that the horrors were rendered just bearable and the whites in his audience would stay with him rather than turn away and close their ears with shame.

On the first evening of the course the co-ordinator dealt with the slave laws of the three main colonisers of the Caribbean — the British, the French and the Spanish — and argued that, by basing their law on the precedent of property law and so denying the humanity of the slave, the British were the cruellest and most ruthless in their treatment of the blacks. That first evening set the tone for the rest of the course. There were no punches pulled. Week after week the group of some twenty whites and ten blacks were presented with the grim details and analyses of the crimes of the white races against the blacks. As promised in the blurb, the course ranged wide, covering history, law, literature and politics and including music, the performance of poetry to bongo drums and visits to two black centres. Speakers included members of black political and self-help groups, a journalist, a political pamphleteer, a teacher, a broadcaster (who was given a very rough time by the black members of the group), a lawyer and a diplomat. There was a lot of debate, some of it heated, but at all times there was a sense of relief, attested to by members of the group, that for once an emotional subject was being treated in a way that recognised the emotion in it. Indeed, some of the whites began responding to the bluntness of the speakers with equal bluntness, challenging generalisations and questioning the usefulness of a political energy fuelled by bitterness.

'I'm not responsible for what happened to your ancestors in the sixteenth century', said one indignant white suddenly. 'Sorry.'

The white liberal's squeamish embarrassment in the presence of the angry black evaporated, and a dialogue developed.

The group asked the institute to continue the course for another term. 'We have got something going here,' one of them said, 'and we can't stop now.' The course ran for another term, the final meeting taking place at the West Indian Students Centre over several glasses of rum. A lot of unlikely people had learnt a lot about each other—a young black woman from New York, an English businessman, a nurse from Granada, the deputy head of a large comprehensive school, a research worker from the Runnymede Trust, a secretary, a man running a black co-operative purchasing scheme...

Academic Detachment

None of the speakers in the 'Black Experience' course conformed to the ideal of the detached academic. They were all invited to put across a committed black point of view, and this fact was featured in the title and the publicity Addison put out about the course. Nor did Addison pay lip service to the concept of academic detachment by appointing a 'neutral' chairman to wrap up each evening with a considered comment designed to put what had been said into an 'acceptable' context. The responsibility for the direction of the course was given to a co-ordinator who was himself thoroughly committed to promulgating an uncompromisingly black point of view.

In setting up the course, Addison was making use of the principle of hearing the story from the horse's mouth. But there was more to it than that. The speakers were not invited simply because they were black and could come into the room and stand there like living case histories and mumble abjectly about their personal experiences. They were campaigners— hard, alert people bent upon changing social attitudes and improving the status of black people and the conditions under which they lived and worked in this country. The course co-ordinator in his amiable way almost never let up, even in casual conversation. Talk to him about painting and he would quickly turn the conversation to black painters. It was obvious that for him the course was simply one more activity in a campaign that involved a whole range of cultural and political activities. He and all the speakers were black and that gave the course its edge. But they were also people striving for change, and that is what made the course hum.

Academics tend to stand apart from change. They distance themselves from their subject, preferring to study and inform rather than act. Some of the academics who had spoken in the 'Race Relations' course the previous year gave this impression very distinctly. But society is in a state of flux, and adult education, being much closer to the ground than most other educational institutions, is in a good position to recognise this fact in its activities. As the 'Black Experience' course demonstrates, there will be times when an adult education centre can usefully set up courses that envisage change as a fact of life and make use of tutors who want a say in what sort of change occurs, people who prefer to devote their energies to playing a part in change rather than simply observing and commenting on it.

Balance

The 'Black Experience' course was thoroughly one-sided. And yet, as it continued, members of the class began reacting, opposing and questioning some of the speakers' assertions. This kind of reaction is a common feature of adult education courses. Once actively involved in the direction of the course, the participants are likely to provide their own 'balance'. This happened at Addision in a course on 'Censorship'. The tutor and guest speakers for the first few meetings worked on the assumption that censorship was undesirable and concerned themselves with how censorship, including self-censorship, was imposed. Most if not all the class were of the same persuasion, but the effect of the presentation was that the class began to agitate for other points of view so that they could begin examining the wider social implications of censorship and the arguments used to justify the limitation of free expression.

In the 'Censorship' course the class demanded a more conventional presentation in which a number of viewpoints could be compared. But the demand for 'balance' can equally well lead to a shift in the other direction. In 1975 Addison ran a course on 'Latin America'. The first few speakers came through the Institute of Latin American Studies in London and were all English academics. For the fifth meeting, however, an Allende supporter who had fled the military junta in Chile was invited. His evening was passionately interesting — an attack on the junta, a chilling description of the coup, particularly as it was effected in the rural areas, and scarifying accusations against the United States and the CIA. Everyone in the room knew his background and his affiliations. No talk could have been more committed to one point of view, and that was the value of it.

After the Chilean's visit members of the group asked me if I could find more speakers who were natives of the countries under discussion and who had a positive political commitment. They wanted the course to move away from the academic and to provide further first-hand accounts of the political turmoil in that part of the world. Since the group asked for the shift I did my best to respond.

There are times when striving for balance can actually militate against education. If two opposing views are constantly put one is tempted into the habit of thinking that the truth must lie between, without really examining either view or the possibility that others exist. If more than two views are put, one is tempted to push a mental button. This one a hit, the rest a miss. But if an adult education course is hard-hitting, if it argues the case, then instead of passively waiting for a counter-argument to be provided the class can adopt the habit of reacting, and in reacting each will take over the ideas as his own or formulate his own in opposition. Learning becomes active.

Objectivity

The 'Black Experience' course was not objective. 'Objectivity' forms a trinity with 'academic detachment' and 'balance'. But one man's objectivity is another man's bias. When someone says: 'Let us look at this objectively' he often means: 'Let us look at this from my point of view'. And in my experience it is those who feel they speak for the majority who make the most use of the word 'objective'.

Complete objectivity is impossible and those who believe they can achieve it are deluding themselves. As soon as people begin discussing a human problem then by definition they cannot be objective because they cannot entirely divest themselves of their own feelings; and the subject, being one to do with people and their behaviour, is not subject to irrefutable measurement. A senior adult educator once avowed that he could speak from the pulpit as a lay preacher on Sunday with all the fervour of his faith, and that on Monday by virtue of his academic training he could conduct a course on a social studies subject with complete objectivity. But is he really able to shrug off his beliefs, his conditioning, his background, the opinions of his friends and enemies, the way last night's dinner is sitting on his stomach, and the thousand and one other factors that will subtly or not so subtly colour the way he teaches, the way he represents others' opinions and the way he leads discussions?

Of course, there will be times when an adult education activity should strive towards objectivity and make use of the tried and tested methods of academic study, but it will be failing to take advantage of its own unique freedoms if it does not make enthusiastic use of non-objective methods as well — if it does not sponsor activities which, like the 'Black Experience' course, take up and build on the emotion, passion and humanity in the subject.

People, not Subjects

One of the most common 'non-objective' methods of course design is to build courses on people rather than disciplines. The adult educator looks for someone who has something interesting or new or exciting or powerful to say and designs the activity around that person, providing the facilities and advice to make the activity educationally viable. We have already seen how this is done in non-controversial subject areas; how a course can be designed round one man's passion for London's history, or based on the skills and inside knowledge a particular professional carpenter possesses.

Addison followed exactly the same principle when setting up the 'Black Experience' course. We had the title — suggested by the principal during a discussion of the shortcomings of the 'Race Relations' course — and we knew we wanted the course to have the pungency of that evening with the black minister, but beyond that we had no very clear idea of what the course would cover or how it should be run. My main concern from the outset was to find the right person to run it. Through an officer of the Community Relations Commission I met the course co-ordinator and once we had agreed the general notion of the course, all I or any other members of Addison's staff really did was provide a context in which the course co-ordinator was able to work. It was he who decided on the subject-matter and it was he who invited the speakers. As a result the course was based almost entirely on his interests, ideas, beliefs, hobby-horses and contacts. Had the officer at the Community Relations Commission suggested another course co-ordinator and had we taken him on, the course would have been very different.

If the adult educator can build a course around an individual who has something interesting or new or exciting or powerful to say, then he can do the same with a group. This is what Addison did in the case of 'Man and Nature' when we handed the running of the course over to a group of London homeopaths. And in handing control of the 'Black Experience' course to the course co-ordinator Addison was in fact also handing it to a group, since the co-ordinator and his speakers almost to a man expressed opinions representative of a specific section of the black community.

Propaganda

But if the adult educator does not seek at every possible turn to ensure academic detachment, balance and objectivity, if he builds his course on people and not on the subject, then surely he is in danger of providing a platform for a group or a particular point of view? Surely the activity he is sponsoring becomes an exercise in propaganda?

'Propaganda' is another of those words. There are some people who would argue that the entire education service is a vehicle for propaganda and that its very reason for existence is to promulgate the standards and views of western industrialised society; that its underlying purpose is to condition people to accept, within quite liberal limits perhaps, one particular way of life. And there are others who seem to label as propaganda any forceful advocacy of a point of view that runs counter to conventional thinking, and as a propagandist anyone who manages to gain more than a momentary hearing. But if we consider the word 'propaganda' in the terms of one group trying to manipulate and subvert others there are certain inherent or easily applied safeguards within adult education that make its exploitation for the purposes of propaganda impossible.

Propaganda is likely to occur when there is coercion, when the students are captive. But coercion does not occur in adult education either in a statutory form or in the more subtle forms associated with voluntary but vocational education. The students are free agents. They attend of their own free will and can walk out at any time. Or, more positively, they can express their difference of opinion by staying and using their influence to counter or change the tenor of the course. The result, as we have seen, is a flexibility and participation alien to the prescribed inflexibility of propaganda.

Propaganda is likely to occur when the right to spontaneous reply is denied. But because there is no coercion and because the students are adults it would be very difficult, if not impossible, to prevent spontaneous comment and criticism in an adult education setting.

Another feature of propaganda is deception. The propagandist does not reveal his true intentions. His aims are covert. It is conceivable that an adult education course could be set up with the intention to deceive, but it is unlikely that the students would tolerate an activity for long if it did not at least start from within the limits defined by the publicity that pulled in the students in the first place. Adult education centres are under the constant scrutiny of their students, who can and do make representations when they feel matters are not as they should be. It is in the interests of the adult education centre to advertise its courses correctly, stating the fact clearly and openly whenever speakers or tutors are employed who will argue from a single, passionately held viewpoint. One can imagine the ructions if the 'Black Experience' course had been advertised as yet another academic study of the sociology of race or as a series of lectures by eminent establishment figures on race relations.

Propaganda flourishes when there is no alternative voice to listen to. But adult education activities tend to provide their own balance. And often an alternative voice will be provided somewhere else within the same adult education programme, providing an option for the student deciding on a course to attend. And even when the adult education programme is a small one and cannot hope to provide a comprehensive reflection of community interests, the course still takes place within the context of a relatively free society in which a wide variety of views and opinions are being expressed through the other sectors of the education service and all the channels of the mass communications media.

The Weak-minded Student

'But what about the weak-minded student?' a fellow adult educator said one day when we were talking along the lines above. This of course is the reduce-everything-to-the-lowest-common-denominator argument, the supreme-caution/risk-nothing argument. Worse, behind this question often lies the arrogance, albeit unconscious arrogance, of the person who is sure he knows what is best for others. After all, who is to decide what constitutes 'weak-minded' or 'readily influenced' or whatever the description is? And who is to decide what these people must be guarded against? Certainly not the adult educator. He is not in the molly-coddling business of primary school education. He is dealing with adults. And if an adult is able to make

his way as a free agent in society at large; if he has run the
gauntlet of doctors, social workers, police, courts, probation
officers and anyone else empowered in any way to cast doubt
on his competence as a human being; if he has made a
voluntary decision to attend a course; and if he has managed
to make it into the classroom, then the assumption must be
that he can look after himself.

Integrity

This does not mean that the adult educator has a free ticket to
unleash on unsuspecting students rabid tutors bent upon
manipulating everyone present; nor that the adult educator can
wash his hands of the whole affair once the course is under
way. Of course he must monitor the activity, and of course he
must very seriously concern himself with the maintenance of
standards.

However, the standards need not be 'academic' ones; the
formulae sometimes used in the other sectors of the education
service do not always apply in adult education. This makes the
adult educator's job not easier but much more difficult
because in the absence of formulae or standard practice he will
have to rely very much on his own judgement with each new
activity he supports, and must often do so in a very fluid
situation.

One of the adult educator's most crucial responsibilities is
the appointment of the tutor. It is also the only point at which
he retains sole control, since once the tutor is appointed the
direction the course takes is subject to the tutor's personal
approach and the wishes of the group that assembles. The
adult educator must make the right choice.

If the adult educator is to sponsor activities that will present
a one-sided case and if he is going to allow tutors free rein and
not impose arbitrary limitations on the content of the course,
then he must do his best to select people of integrity. But by
'integrity' I do not want to imply conformity to a set of
accepted attitudes, even though they be high ones. I mean
people honest to themselves and their own beliefs *and genuinely respectful of others*. The co-ordinator of the 'Black
Experience' course was just such a person. He was fired by a
desire to convince people of the justness of his cause (and the

justification for his anger) but he was respectful of other people and their opinions. He wanted to test his views against all comers and demonstrate how unassailable they were. His technique was to argue from one passionately held point of view—and invite it to be contested. He would have seen no point in taking advantage of someone's weakness.

Wisdom

Naturally the adult educator must ensure that the tutor knows his subject, for a tutor who really knows his subject also knows how people react to his subject and has an understanding of the way in which his field of knowledge fits into the broader scheme of things. He is sure of himself. His knowledge of his subject gives him a confidence that goes beyond the subject and no matter how passionately involved he is in his field or how eager he is to persuade people of the justness of his cause, he is calm, serene even. The adult educator responsible for the 'New Philosophy' courses at Central Wandsworth Institute used the word, and he was right to: in appointing tutors the adult educator should look for men and women who are *wise*.

Quality

In his supervision of the course and the advice he gives to the tutor the adult educator must seek to ensure the quality of the activity. Quality is something he must sense in the atmosphere of the classroom. He will see it in the students' faces and the ease with which the tutor performs his job. He will sense it in the way a disparate group of adults gells for the evening. Earlier I used the word 'hum'. The organiser of the 'New Philosophy' courses used the word 'glow'. Quality in an adult education activity is impossible to describe in any truly satisfactory way, but it is easy enough to detect when it is there.

In trying to identify this quality I want to start with two things it is not, and then describe three factors that may play a part in bringing it about.

Quality in adult education has nothing to do with whether a course is for beginners or advanced students. A course for illiterate adults in the very basics of reading and writing and a course for literate adults on the finer points of Blake's poetry may operate at different levels, but both activities can be profoundly illuminating experiences and both subjects will require considerable educational skill on the part of the tutors if they are to be taught well. In the adult education world an odd snobbery prevails, based upon the assumption that the 'higher' the level of the course in conventional academic terms, the greater the skill required of the tutor and the more worthy the activity in general. This snobbery can be seen reflected in the difference in rates of pay. All too often the tutor taking the practical activity or the course based on local affairs is paid less than the tutor taking the 'academic' activity or the activity that looks at broader, more 'universal' issues.

The worst example of this confusion of level with quality can often be found in the teaching of English as a second language. Here the tutors of beginners' classes are often paid less than the tutors of the more advanced levels, on the assumption, one imagines, that teaching a beginners' class requires less effort and skill than teaching a higher level. But if anything the opposite is the case, since the gruelling business of teaching the basics of English to a group of adults with no common language requires a specialised knowledge and certain skills and gifts not necessary at the higher levels where a grounding of the language has already been established.

But to reverse the mistake and imply that teaching language at the lower levels is the more worthy activity is equally wrong. In an adult education activity, quality is unrelated to the level of teaching or study or work pursued. Indeed there are times in adult education when the concept of levels becomes meaningless. Was the 'Black Experience' course, for example, equivalent in content and work done to an 'O' level course or an 'A' level course, or was it at the level of a university course perhaps? The course adopted such non-academic procedures that any attempt to find a place for it in the conventional scheme of levels would be impossible.

Nor does quality in an adult education activity have anything to do with whether the subject-matter is 'popular' or 'classical'. A course on rock music can be as stimulating, as musically informed and socially informative, as mind-opening an experience as a course built round a study of the symphonies of Beethoven (although this last statement might arouse outraged protest in some quarters). Again I do not want to replace one snobbery with another and imply that the 'popular' is somehow better source material than the 'classical'. The point is that the quality we are looking for is not necessarily dictated by the academic respectability or otherwise of the subject-matter.

The trouble in assessing the standard of an adult education activity is that one is often tempted to look *outside* the activity, comparing it with what is being done in the other sectors of the education service or attempting to measure it against some set of absolute criteria. But adult education is so different that comparison with the other sectors will often mislead rather than help. And adults tend to demand of an adult education activity such a personal relevance that appeals to any set of absolute criteria will often become pointless. So perhaps it would be better to look *within* the activity itself and resist the temptation to make comparisons with other superficially similar activities elsewhere.

Quality in adult education does have a lot to do with appropriateness. An adult education activity should be appropriate to the moment, the subject, the community, the people involved. An evening dressmaking class in a fully equipped dressmaking room in a purpose-built adult education centre drawing its students from all four corners of a wide catchment area will differ enormously from a dressmaking class held in a community hall on Tuesday afternoons on a run-down housing estate and attended only by women from that estate. The teaching methods the tutors adopt and the goals they and their students set themselves will in all likelihood be very different. The afternoon tutor may teach short-cuts that would horrify the evening tutor. The end products—a lovingly created holiday frock to be worn in the Canary Islands and a dress for a four-year-old put together in an afternoon—may simply not bear comparison. The children underfoot in the afternoon class on the estate will make a difference. And indeed the afternoon tutor may not even be 'qualified' in the conventional terms. She may have been chosen because of her community qualifications as much as her ability to teach, because she lives on the estate herself and understands from personal experience the requirements of her students, because she knows them and can give them what they want. And yet there is no reason to assume that either the afternoon or the evening class will automatically be a better adult education activity than the other.

Quality is to be found in the striving within the adult education activity rather than in the standard of the finished product. Too often we judge an educational activity by what comes out at the end of it—the pot, the dress, the short story—and fail to take into account the value of the human experience within the activity itself. Many adult education centres support brass bands, providing rehearsal space and paying the band's director as tutor. Some of these bands could stand comparison with the best in the land but others most certainly could not, and an outsider listening to a brass band playing a medley of airs, complete with discordant fluffs and two false starts, at a neighbourhood carnival on a summer Saturday afternoon could be forgiven for finding the experience less than impressive. But of course that medley at the carnival is not the whole story. Had the outsider known that the personnel of the band were drawn entirely from the neighbourhood; had he attended the rehearsals and witnessed the intensity with which the band prepared for the performance; had he watched the director and the section leaders striving to bring the newcomers up to the level of the rest of the band; had he shared the band's realisation at the eleventh hour that in one piece they had set their sights too high and that they would have to leave it out of Saturday's programme; and had he not been an outsider at all, but the father of a seventeen-year-old newcomer to the cornet section, then in all likelihood he would have agreed that the activity as a whole had a very special quality largely unassociated with the excellence or otherwise of that one performance.

Perhaps most important of all, quality in an adult education activity is associated with pleasure. In 1974 a colleague from another London institute phoned me at Addison and recommended a tutor in astrology. After getting a tentative go-ahead from my principal I met the tutor. The tutor was clearly deeply involved in his subject and intent upon sharing his knowledge. But there was nothing of the proselytiser about him. He was softly spoken, and had the ability and willingness to listen as well as talk. And his smile, usually accompanied by a small positive nod of the head, was easy and extraordinarily outwardgoing. I liked him immediately and upon my recommendation astrology was included in our 1974-5 programme. But as the time for the course approached I became increasingly aware of the fact that I had based my support for the course more on my liking of the tutor than on my knowledge of the subject. I was also mildly worried by a recent conversation with the tutor. He had said that he would have to deluge his students with printed notes and tables of calculations at the outset of the course and count on them doing a considerable amount of private study. This, I feared, smacked a little of the inexperienced tutor's over-eagerness to get on with the subject, the expert's inability to treat beginners as beginners. Because of these doubt I fully intended to sit in on the first meeting, but the pressures of the beginning of the year took me to other branches and classes and it was only in the third week that I went to the astrology class, and then only half-way through the evening. The tea-break was under way and the canteen was crowded with students. I saw the astrology tutor standing near the canteen counter and went up to him. He greeted me and took me over to the tables where his group was sitting. People looked up and the impression was immediate and complete. Every person there was pleased. They were pleased with the course. They were pleased with the tutor. They were pleased with themselves. Their faces glowed with that deep, satisfying pleasure that comes with the adventure of really learning something. I followed the group into the classroom but that almost tangible sense of pleasure coming from the students had already told me that the course must be a good one.

The 'Black Experience' course was a non-academic course, but I believe it had this quality I have tried to identify. It was appropriate to the time (I doubt if the same form of course would be appropriate now, six years on), it was appropriate to the area, and to the interests and requirements of the people who attended. There was a sense of striving in the course, an urgent desire on the part of those present to come to grips with a complex human issue and establish some common ground. And if the mood of the group at the end of first term when they asked that the course be extended is anything to go by, then the course succeeded in giving them real and valuable pleasure.

Value-loaded Concepts

Integrity, wisdom and quality are concepts that are felt, not measured, and so defy satisfactory description. They are value-loaded concepts. In this discussion I have tried to replace academic detachment, balance and objectivity with integrity, wisdom and quality as yardsticks by which to judge an adult education activity. Academic detachment, balance and objectivity are value-loaded concepts that masquerade as something else. At least integrity, wisdom and quality have the virtue of being openly value-loaded. If we use them we are less likely to be dogmatic. We are more likely to be aware that assessing, applying and maintaining standards in adult education is a tricky, thoroughly subjective business.

Chapter 23

Community Action

Learning by Doing

An adult education course dealing with a social problem will
be strangely lacking if it does not engage in, or lead to, or at
least point the way to action. It would be unsatisfactory to talk
of the inhospitable environment of a housing estate without in
the same breath considering ways of putting things right.
Indeed abstract or detached analysis by itself will not be
tolerated for long by a group of adults all of whom come from
a single area or identifiable community. Very soon they will
begin agitating for the course to shift from generalities to
specifics, and for what they are learning to be demonstrated as
relevant to them and their own situation. And very often this
demand for relevance will be accompanied by a demand for
action. The students will begin asking: 'What can we *do*?'

This move from the general to the specific and then to
action occurred in a civil liberties course run at Addison. The
tutor came from the other side of London, while the students
were for the most part drawn from Hammersmith. They
included a retired builder who wanted 'to get involved in
community work in some way', a shop steward working at
Olympia exhibition hall, a young woman working with the
Hammersmith Council for Community Relations, two solici-
tor's clerks, a middle-aged woman, a man in his late twenties
working in market research, a man intending to go into local
politics — about fifteen people in all. The course was planned
for ten meetings and the tutor presented a fairly 'standard'
course covering police powers of search and arrest, bail,
courts, tribunals, freedom of speech and censorship. But as the

course continued the group increasingly sought to relate the issues being discussed to the local context—just how easy or difficult was it to get bail in the local magistrates' court compared with the courts in other parts of London, for example; and at the end of the term ten of the group decided to continue meeting and to poll an area of Hammersmith in order to ascertain how aware people were of the various sources of legal advice. The tutor withdrew, saying that the only role he could usefully play in this local survey was that of occasional adviser; and the class took on the form of a detached action-research group, with the institute providing minor administrative support, helping find and pay one or two advisers on request, and duplicating the group's report. Not surprisingly when one looks at the make-up of the group, the report, entitled *Public Awareness of Primary Sources of Legal Advice*, was a good one. And the activity as a whole was a good example of how adults often prefer to learn by doing, how they often want to take action.

Organisation, Development and Action
By the mid 1970s ILEA was beginning to face up to the fact that the policy of outreach was involving some of its adult education institutes in community action. In early 1977 the authority circulated to all institute academic boards and governing bodies a discussion document entitled *The Educational Approach to Controversial Learning Situations*. In a later chapter (p.222) I describe how this paper came to be written, but for the moment I want to quote from paragraph 7:

> In the design of their programme institutes have always sought to respond to the shifting pattern of interests and aspirations in the surrounding community. With the introduction of outreach work the institutes have involved themselves more actively in the affairs of their communities. It has been recognised that this active approach, this attempt to stimulate and encourage learning situations in the manner and place where they will best flourish, is a valid educational role for the institutes to engage in. Here it may be helpful to recognise three aspects of this kind of work:
> (i) 'Community organisation', in which the professional

decides provision and in the case of adult education designs the activity and, within the normal give and take of any adult education activity, retains control.

(ii) 'Community development', in which the clients participate in the planning and the professionals, where they exist, act as catalysts and advisers. In the case of adult education this would involve throwing out ideas and providing facilities and expert advice on method, but exercising no more control over the content and direction of the learning activity than any other participant.

(iii) 'Community action', when community feeling has developed and a group of people actively engage in a living community situation to affect that situation and achieve a particular end. It needs to be recognised, however, that there may come a point when the educational agency will no longer be needed to promote the learning situation.

Dosser Power

The phrase 'community action' can evoke strong images of rabid people taking to the streets, dumping rubbish on the town hall steps and publicly debagging a brace of councillors, or at least locking a few of them into a community hall overnight. But community action can be, and usually is, much quieter than that. It can consist, for example, of a group of dossers gathering together and, over a number of weeks, gradually writing a joint letter . . . .

One of those London outreach workers, working out of the City Literary Institute, began dropping in on Thursday afternoons at the Kingsway day centre, a centre frequented by down-and-outs, dossers and hostel-dwellers. 'I found it difficult and strange at first' he said. 'They didn't know how to treat me and I didn't know how to treat them.' But he continued going each Thursday afternoon, chatting to various regulars and gradually getting to know them. Out of this developed a weekly gathering of up to fifteen regulars. Normally the day centre closed at 3.30, but the worker arranged with the day centre staff to meet with his 'discussion group' and stay on for another hour. The discussions were none too formal. Some of those staying on took part in the discussion from the billiard table, playing and occasionally throwing in some comment. The outreach worker made no attempt to steer the discussion in any predetermined direction, but simply asked questions and listened. For the most part the group talked of themselves, of their condition, of the way they lived, of the hostels many of them spent their nights in.

After a number of meetings the outreach worker invited his group to the City Literary Institute nearby, suggesting they might want to record something on video tape. They came, some wearing ties, hair spruced for the occasion, into the City Literary Institute building, mingling with the institute's students of literature, languages, music and drama. They recorded a discussion, one man interviewed some of the others, one read some poetry, another imitated Charlie Chaplin. The outreach worker took the recorder and monitor to the day centre the following week and the tape was shown to anyone interested in seeing it. But there was no reaction. 'It was strange' the outreach worker said. 'A lot of men sat around waiting to see the tape, but then they just watched in silence.'

Perhaps it was because the tape failed to make any particular point effectively, because it failed to communicate in any detail the substance of the group's previous meetings, that the group decided to put something down on paper. But rather than record a statement the group decided to write a protest letter and send it to some of the people they felt held sway over their lives. It was the outreach worker's hand that held the pen, but he recorded each point only after discussion and with the full agreement of the group, so that although the syntax may have been his, the letter was as far as he could make it a true expression of the group's ideas and feelings and not a do-gooding outsider's interpretation.

This is the final text the group decided upon and which they sent to the chairman of the Westminster City Council, the council's housing department manager, the director of the council's social services, and the warden of a hostel where many of the users of the day centre spent their nights:

We write to you as a group of men who use Kingsway Day Centre and who have been discussing our circumstances. We want our voice to be heard.

Those of us who use — — House are disgusted at the conditions there. The toilets are not fit for human use, and nobody bothers to clear the pigeon mess from the tables where we eat. If such conditions are put down to the fault of the people who use — — House, we want to point out that our Day Centre has much cleaner toilets, and the conditions at some other hostels are much better — yet the same type of people use these places.

We also want to say that a lot of the problems of hostels are caused because they *are* hostels. Why do we have to live in hostels year-in, year-out, with our social security benefits geared to hostel rates? These hostels were intended for emergencies, but are full of 'regulars' who book in week after week. But they are not designed for regular lodging, and we keep out others with emergency needs. What you have done is turn us into hostel dwellers and forced us to adopt a way of life you disapprove of. What we need is decent accommodation suitable for single persons to live in, with some independence and self-respect. Some of the Day Centre people have recently become tenants in a short-life house. The property has not been turned into a slum, nor wrecked, nor burnt down. But because of our present circumstances, people do not want us as neighbours, and do not want to give us lodgings. There are very few bedsitters going, and landlords demand something like £60 deposit and £40 rent in advance. We do not have that kind of money, and even if we had we should still find it hard to get anywhere.

There are not large armies of us in London. About 200 people use this Day Centre regularly, and perhaps another 100 come in some time during the year. That is not a vast amount of people to find lodging for, especially when you look at the number of empty houses around. Why cannot more of these be used?

We are writing to ask you if better arrangements can be urgently made at — — House. We also wish to learn if Westminster has any plans to make accommodation available for single people wanting to get out of the 'hostel' ditch. What proportion of housing in the City is for single people? Can single people get on the waiting list, with any hope of something? Have you any long-term plans that will help us?

One problem remained. How were they to sign it? No one wanted to put their name to it since they felt so dependent for their day-to-day survival on those they were criticising. They discussed the problem for some time and finally decided to sign the letter 'Thursdays at 3.30'.[33]

Drawing the Line

There are some adult educators who would claim that in helping the dossers write their protest letter the outreach worker went too far. They would argue that an adult educator should certainly engage in community organisation (the setting up and provision of courses), that there will be times when he can legitimately play a part in community development (by providing a course in a particular location or with a particular group or section of the community in mind), but that he should under no circumstances engage in community action.

In simple terms this argument says that it is right and proper for an adult educator to run a course on citizens' rights, but that he should not actually help the students obtain those rights. Or that it is within his brief to provide a course for a tenants' association on 'how to run a meeting' but that he must withdraw as soon as the meetings begin to achieve anything. Or that, in the case of the dossers, it was all right for the outreach worker to walk into the day centre and get the discussions going; it was all right for him to help the dossers develop a group consciousness and begin making a critical examination of their situation; it was all right for him to help them make the tape and show it at the day centre in the hope of drawing others into their group experience; but that once the dossers had embarked on the letter and it ceased to be a record of their findings and became an instrument for protest then the outreach worker should have withdrawn his active support.

This argument may at first glance seem to provide a neat solution to the problem of how far an adult educator should involve himself and his centre in the community, but as paragraph 7 of *The Educational Approach to Controversial*

Learning Situations points out, life is not like that:

> It must be stressed, however, that the above [community organisation, community development, community action] are only aspects of a complex community process. It is in fact impossible to draw clear lines between the aspects or assume that any particular one must precede or follow any one of the others. Action groups might form before the event and seek help from an institute in preparing and informing themselves for a coming crisis, but it is equally likely that they will come together and seek assistance in the heat of the crisis itself, then go on after initial action to reorganise themselves and prepare for the next round. Another group might seek institute support in a non-controversial community development project but be projected rapidly into action by a sudden turn of events, or even come to the realisation through the help provided by the institute that action is necessary. The institute itself might set up an activity based on the study of a social issue and find that it has given birth to an action group. The institute will even from time to time find itself engaged directly in action itself as an inevitable result of its own activities, as in the case of providing information on rights to those who have been denied the information.

In other words, in real-life organisation, development and action get jumbled up.

But far more important, the argument that one must draw the line at action forgets that there are human beings involved.

To engage in community education work with the intention of retreating at the first sign of action would be extraordinarily callous. The adult educator must remember that he is entering into other people's lives. He is seeking to win their trust and to prove the value of the educational experience he is providing. If he succeeds at all he will begin raising their hopes, and it is precisely at that delicate moment when a group of people have developed enough confidence in themselves to contemplate action with some hope of success that the adult educator must give them all the support that he can. Imagine the loss of faith, the anger and bitterness, the seriously destructive effect it could have had on those dossers if, having got this group of dispirited people at the fag-end of society to begin lifting up their heads, the outreach worker had suddenly felt obliged to act in accordance with some formula and let them drop. The dossers would have seen no logic in his actions, just a simple and devastating case of desertion.

Education as the Yardstick

But the adult educator's brief remains educational and education remains his yardstick in judging the extent to which he can involve himself and his centre in the affairs of the community. The adult educator may find his activities running alongside community action, arising out of it, spawning it or inextricably intermixed with it, and he should not be frightened of that. The question he should ask himself is not whether the activity involves community action, but whether the activity as a whole is still educational. While it is, he should stay with it.

Gone is the seductively neat formula, the escape clause allowing the adult educator to make a bolt for the door as soon as the activity becomes controversial. Now he must make difficult subjective judgements. But although the problem may seem new because it is 'out there' in the community and no longer neatly contained in a classroom, it is in principle no different from the problem facing the adult educator in deciding whether to continue providing facilities for the Inland Revenue Badminton Club. As we have already seen, a lot of adult education centres support local clubs engaged in non-controversial activities such as badminton, bridge, or studying local history, giving them a regular slot in their programme, providing accommodation and often paying a member of the group as the tutor. Many of the activities go on year in, year out, and what the adult educator must ask himself each time he renews his support is whether what the club is doing is still educational. Are those people from the Inland Revenue offices down the road who occupy the top hall every Thursday evening still learning to play badminton or are they simply gathering together for a couple of hours of relaxation? And what about the advanced bridge group? Not the beginners' class further down the corridor but that lot in there who simply seem to be playing?

And what about the dossers? They may have begun to take action, but was the activity as a whole still educational? Surely it was only with the introduction of an element of action that a wandering, hesitant series of discussions actually became a genuinely educational activity? When the dossers realised they could write the letter and send it to people who mattered, the discussions became meaningful, searching, critical. Their meetings now had a purpose. They were learning about themselves and the agencies that controlled their lives. They were investigating their relationship with those agencies and contemplating how it could be changed. They were working together, getting to know each other and about each other rather than just co-existing in the same miserable space. They were discovering that they could actually do something themselves. They were lifting up their heads. For my money, what they were doing once they began writing that letter was quintessentially educational.

Courting Community Activists

If education and action can go hand in hand, then it seems perfectly reasonable that the adult educator should actually seek out community activists and offer to provide them with educational support. Thus he might organise a course on alternative education for a group contemplating setting up a free school, enabling them to study the project in detail and hear from others who have gone before them of the various possibilities and pitfalls. Or he might run courses on the environment and the techniques of community action for a group concerned with combating local waste of resources. Or he might offer a course on local government procedures as support information to groups demanding more play space and follow that up with a course on playgroup and adventure playground leadership. In other words the adult educator should always be on the lookout for opportunities to make educational capital out of living community situations.

Nor is there much likelihood that by adopting this pro-activist policy the adult educator will find himself consorting with rowdies and hotheads. Joining an adult education course requires serious commitment; and the ranters and ravers and the butterflies are soon sorted out since there is little point in coming back the next week unless one really wants to learn.

It is equally unlikely that the adult educator will find himself providing support for action that is unrealistic. Adult education students, whether activists or not, are part-time, and must take what is learnt back into their everyday lives. Other educational institutions create artificial worlds in which everyday pressures, against which ideas will eventually have to be tested, are removed. But in adult education, conclusions reached must match up to reality since they jostle for the rest of the week with the student's real life. Community action decided upon under these conditions is likely to be well-judged, well-informed and as a result more effective.

Since 1970 Addison has run a group of some twenty-five special studies courses each year. They have all in some way or another attempted to expand on the institute's regular programme, and a number of them have always dealt with social or community issues. They have been 'formal' courses to the extent that most of them have been set up on the institute's initiative, and most have been held on institute premises. They have included courses on:

Civil liberties
Planning and community action
Population, resources, environment
Crime and the community
Welfare Rights
Community arts
Homosexuality: changing attitudes
Alternative education
Black experience
Housing
Mental illness
Community self-help
Power and authority
Censorship
Working with the out-of-work

The aim of all these courses has been to alert people to social problems and to attract them into a classroom where they can study them and consider ways of putting them right. In its special studies programme Addison has been courting, and seeking to create, community activists.

Chapter 24

Responsibilities

Active Role

In their community work adult educators have an 'active' and a 'passive' role to play. In their active role it is they who make the move. It is they who approach community groups suggesting ways in which their centre might help. Their choice of groups will be arbitrary. They will choose groups they like, that they think they can help educationally, or that they believe have something educationally valuable to say. And they are perfectly justified in making these choices, since they have been appointed by their masters as professional educators with the responsibility for doing just that and because with such limited resources at their disposal they would be unable to offer support to everyone in any event.

It was just such an arbitrary decision on the part of that outreach worker at the City Lit to approach those dossers; and in a more formal context, it was just such an arbitrary decision on Addison's part to offer educational support to the Hammersmith Association for Mental Health . . . .

Mental Stress

The Hammersmith Association for Mental Health was set up in late 1972 with the aim of co-ordinating community concern for the care, particularly the after-care, of the mentally ill and in order to bring pressure to bear on the responsible authorities. The association was composed of local doctors, lawyers, churchmen and other men and women, mainly middle-class, who devoted a good amount of their spare time to voluntary work. In 1973 I approached the association's executive committee suggesting that Addison and the association co-operate in order to set up a course on the subject of mental stress. The association agreed and appointed a sub-committee made up of a consultant psychiatrist, a GP and a social worker, who together designed a ten-meeting course dealing with the concepts of mental illness, the types of causes, the methods of treatment, and the provision by friends, family and community of after-care. I attended two meetings of this sub-committee and suggested the inclusion of one subject and one speaker, but apart from that played no part in the syllabus design and simply offered advice on the broad structure of the course.

The course, chaired by the consultant psychiatrist and making use of a number of guest speakers, ran for ten meetings. From Addison's point of view it provided another successful slot in our overall programme, but from the association's point of view the course served several purposes beyond that. The course was held a year after the association had been formed and, at a time when first enthusiasms might have been flagging, was able to provide a brief focal point for the association's activities. In all its publicity Addison announced the course as being 'organised in conjunction with the Hammersmith Association for Mental Health', so the course served as an advertisement of the association's existence. The course served as a form of 'in-service' training for some of the members of the association, enabling them to consider in detail some of the problems their association was grappling with. And since the course drew in a good number of students from beyond the association's membership, it served a source of possible recruitment. Indeed the final meeting was led by the organiser of the Hammersmith volunteer bureau, and resulted in a number of the students deciding to form a befrienders group for people recently discharged from mental hospital. The association found itself with a number of new members prepared to train themselves and add a new dimension to the association's activities.

To sum up, then, Addison approached the association in the first place, let it design and run the course, openly publicised the relationship, and allowed the course to be used for recruitment. But I doubt if anyone would object to any of that.

It is part of adult education's function to initiate courses. It is right and proper for a centre to do this in conjunction with and for the benefit of a genuine community group. We were confident of the credentials of the people the association appointed to run the course. And if the association used the course as a platform from which to promote its cause, and as a recruiting post in order to swell its ranks, well, that was all right too, since the association may have been a pressure group but its aims were thoroughly respectable.

One Uncomfortable Evening
The only unconventional aspect of the course was introduced by the institute, in the form of the speaker I suggested. She had been a founder member of People Not Psychiatry, a movement that grew up in the late 1960s based on the teaching of Reich, Laing and Cooper and whose stance, encapsulated in the organisation's name, was an opposition to conventional psychiatry as practised in the hospitals. I had invited her to an earlier course, and she had spoken with force and warmth and disturbing good reason. By the time we were planning the 'Mental Stress' course, my speaker and her daughter had moved north to live in a commune along with several friends drawn together by their interest in Reichian therapy. I wrote to her and she hitch-hiked down to London to speak at the fourth meeting of the course.

The meeting went badly from the start. She set out to give a very personal statement, drawing upon her own experience and describing the way in which she and the other members of the commune worked and employed some of the techniques of Reichian therapy in their everyday lives. She did not attack conventional psychiatric practice directly, although obviously everything she said was based upon the belief that there were alternatives, and she was careful to describe what she felt were her areas of competence and what were not; but perhaps because I had mentioned her association with PNP, perhaps because of her initially relaxed and informal manner and the directness with which she looked at and spoke to individuals in the room, and perhaps because she was dressed simply, three of the students seemed to treat everything she said with open hostility, interrupting her, not letting her finish making a point before attacking, even talking to each other across the room referring to the speaker in the third person. It was discourteous behaviour of the sort I had not seen before in an adult education setting, and the speaker had trouble dealing with it. Indeed, she tightened up so much that I thought we might have to abandon the meeting. But then, with a visible effort she relaxed, waited for an attack to peter out, looked up and in an electric moment asked the three people why they were so hostile. The question stopped them short and the speaker proceeded to talk out her personal reactions to their hostility and the way they had expressed it, and to describe her feelings as she was experiencing them there and then. She linked this up with the way tension was dealt with in the commune, how in a Reichian therapy session tension was built upon as something valuable and positive, how they believed that by treating tension with drugs one was damping down or dissipating a potentially valuable energy... and the evening continued. But the hostility of those three had silenced the others and there was no discussion, so that the speaker found herself in the situation—probably alien to everything she believed in—of delivering a lecture. Towards the end of the evening the three re-opened their attack, spurred on by the revelation that the speaker subsisted on supplementary bene- fits and picking upon her quite amiable admission that her teenage daughter was in the process of adopting a thoroughly conventional life-style in open reaction to the unconvention- ality of her mother.

At the end of the meeting the speaker left the room ahead of most of the class. I joined her, conscious of the fact that she had been through an unpleasant experience and that it was I who had invited her into it. As we went down the stairs I began apologising, but was cut short by a voice behind us. One of the members of the group, a woman in her late twenties, was running after us. She came up to the speaker, speaking rapidly: 'You were wonderful. Everything you said was fasci- nating. I didn't know what to say in there but I want to tell you your talk was terrific.'

Another member of the group joined us, saying much the same. The speaker began laughing with relief. By the time we were out of the building several others had joined us and we

stood on the pavement outside, laughing and talking. Someone suggested a drink and we went to the nearest pub. There I
began apologising again, but the speaker interrupted me,
saying: 'It's all right. I had a feeling the evening would end
well.'

The evening with the speaker from the commune was a
break in the course, but no more than that. The other evenings
were presented by practising professionals in the fields of
psychiatric medicine, social work and aftercare, all of whom
were invited by the sub-committee and all of whom put across
mainstream points of view. It was, including that one uncomfortable evening, a valuable activity for the institute to have
put on.

'Passive' Role

When I approached the Hammersmith Association for Mental
Health I was the initiator of the idea. I was playing an active
role. But the adult educator has a 'passive' role to play in his
relationships to the community as well. As we have seen, adult
education is based in principle and to a large extent in
practice, on response to demand. And word gets around. In
performing his active role of offering support to specific
groups, or aiming his courses at specific sectors of the community, the adult educator is inevitably broadcasting the fact
that he has resources that can be used. And in the courses he
puts on he is effectively demonstrating *how* his resources can
be used. In 1977 Addison received a letter from a local resident
asking for a course on Irish studies. He suggested a series of ten
or twelve lectures attacking prejudice against the Irish and
covering topics such as Irish history, culture, archaeology,
literature, music and current affairs. The course structure he
proposed was a replica of the 'Black Experience' course, and
towards the end of his letter he said: 'Surely if there are courses
on West Indian studies there should also be courses on Irish
studies, especially in areas such as ours?'

The institute set about arranging the course.

But what would Addison have done if, instead of being
approached by an individual seriously concerned with combating ignorance and prejudice, we had been approached by a
group of political extremists? And what would we have done if

this group of political extremists had cited the example of the 'Mental Stress' course and demanded that we provide them with a platform in exactly the same way as we had unreservedly provided a platform (and recruiting post) for the Hammersmith Association for Mental Health?

Of course one man's extremism is another man's norm, but let us assume for the moment that I am talking about a group who advocated wholesale and bloody revolution or a group who advocated wholesale suppression of basic freedoms laced with racism. What would we do if either of these groups approached us, demanding a course dealing exclusively with their preoccupations, activities and beliefs?

As in the case of the bingo red herring, there are two answers to this. The first is that it does not happen, or at least that to my knowledge it has not happened in the blunt, unequivocal way I have suggested it could. And perhaps that is significant. Perhaps that is because political extremists are by definition people who have little desire to expend the effort and time it takes to run and attend a series of meetings of a carefully limited number of people at which every point can be contested, disputed at length and at the end of the day quite possibly rejected. Political extremists are probably more interested in demagogy, or in small groups that they are reasonably sure they can control. They are probably less likely to want to act in conjunction with an institution that, while not wanting to censor what the extremists have to say, would retain strict control over the context in which they said it; that would insist on the affiliations of the speakers being publicised in advance, enrolment being voluntary and every member of the group having the right to immediate reply or to call for an alternative viewpoint. Perhaps the real definition of an extremist is a person in whom destructive thinking outweighs constructive thinking. To such a person an adult education activity with all its safeguards in operation would probably be too alien an activity to contemplate.

And supposing an adult education centre did put on a course presenting an extreme political point of view and advertised it openly as such, then in all likelihood it would be attended not only by people wanting to hear the extremists, but by people eager to put the views of the extremists to the test. In such a case, if the ideas expressed were valid, then their validity would be demonstrated in a running debate in which the advocates of the ideas would be seen to be able to hold their own under attack; and if the views were indeed those of the fanatic, then they would be stripped bare and exposed as fanaticism by people attracted to the course for the express purpose of doing just that.

But none of this sounds very educational. It all sounds rather too much like reinforcement on the one hand or conflict on the other. And that brings me to the second answer to the question of what a centre would do if approached by a group of political extremists, and again it echoes the answer to the bingo red herring. It is, of course, that the adult educator is not obliged to respond willy-nilly to any and every demand from any and every group in his area. He is not there to give away rooms and money and let himself and his centre be used without restriction. He is an educator and his response must be educational.

Two-way Transaction

When a group asks for support in order to state their case or plead their cause they are asking to enter into a two-way transaction. They may want to use the centre's resources, but in accepting the centre's support they are also accepting that the adult educator will in his turn want to make use of them. What they are doing in effect is offering their ideas, their personnel and their beliefs as a resource, around which the adult educator, using his knowledge of method, will attempt to build a valuable educational activity.

In such a two-way transaction, the adult educator is the professional educator, the expert on method. Obviously he will design the activity in consultation with the applicant group, but it will be he who has the final say on the site, the length of the course, the maximum size of the group, the balance between lecture and discussion, and the style of publicity.

The answer to the question of who has the final say on the subject-matter is much less clear. After all, we are talking about *adult* education, and the adult educator is taking on a great deal if he assumes the right to say what adults may or may not discuss in a centre ostensibly there to serve those adults. Of course there will be legal restrictions on what can be said or advocated. Adult education is not outside the law. Inciting people to racial violence, inciting people to commit a crime, is illegal. Courses on bomb-making, or ten-meeting hate sessions against black people are not on. But if it remains within the law, the subject-matter alone does not justify refusing the demand for a course. After all, if refused point-blank our group of political extremists would have every justification in asking pointedly why it was all right to offer a platform to the Hammersmith Association for Mental Health (or the Christian Community at Temple Lodge, or the 'Black Experience' crowd) but not to them.

Challenge

The temptation for adult educators is to run scared, to scuttle behind the skirts of the other sectors of the education service and have nothing to do with groups that engage in controversial thought and action, arguing that if the other sectors do not offer these groups a platform then they must not either. But this is to deny the unique character of adult education. This is to deny its freedoms and safeguards and the fact that an adult education centre with its relaxed, untrendy atmosphere and sense of co-operative endeavour is as near perfect a setting as you could hope to find for the study of a controversial topic.

In their active approach to community groups, adult educators are looking for groups they can help and for groups round which they can build valuable educational activities. In their 'passive' role, in their response to unsolicited demands, they should continue the search. If a group seeks their support or wants to make use of their resources, they should regard the request as a challenge. Will they be able to build into a course run by this group the educational objectives of learning, productive social contact, self-discovery, and the raising of the individual's self-esteem? Will they be able to guarantee the safeguards of honest publicity, voluntary enrolment, right to spontaneous reply and available alternative voices? Can they find from within the group a tutor of knowledge and integrity? In short, will the course be one of quality?

These conditions, when listed together, appear to be a tall

order, but one-sided adult education courses run by groups
with sectarian or political or mystical or philosophical or
community affiliations can be and have been genuinely educational.

An IRA Course?

Bombs explode in Belfast. People are blown to pieces, or have
a leg or an arm torn off, or are disfigured or blinded or
deafened or paralysed, or rendered idiots or living vegetables.
Others are abducted, tortured, hooded and 'executed'. Have I,
sitting here in West London constructing arguments on paper,
talked myself into the hypothetical situation of supporting a
request from a local group of IRA sympathisers for a course
that would plead the IRA cause? Have I talked myself into
supporting a course that would advocate murder?

The answer is no. I have not talked myself into this
particular corner, since such a group or course would not meet
my tall order. But it would be unwise to rush on, feeling
smugly that we had dealt with this problem. It is my belief that
the nightmare of Northern Ireland is behind the current
uncertainty in a lot of people's minds, particularly those trying
to pursue liberal or radical policies in the public arena. Often
the subject is repressed, not voiced, perhaps not even consciously recognised as being relevant to issues we all face, but
Northern Ireland *is* there and it *is* relevant. Whenever we
attempt to push our freedoms a little further we have to face
up to the likely consequences of these advances in the light of
Northern Ireland. Remove the controls that still muzzle our
press, and we suddenly have to ask what that might mean in
relation to the Northern Ireland extremists. Argue for an
increase in local community control in the form of neighbourhood councils and community action and we have to ask what
that might mean in a divided Belfast. Argue for access to our
television networks by local community and political groups
and we have to face up to what access to television, or truly
local neighbourhood radio and television, might mean in
Northern Ireland.

Northern Ireland produces the horror questions, the dilem-
mas that make people seeking radical solutions retreat. The
situation casts its negative shadow over the whole country,

making people who might otherwise push a cause as far as it will logically go, hesitate and hold back because they are aware that in one part of the country their arguments and reasoning might be taken up by certain people who no longer observe even the minimum constraints of civilised society. I watched from the sidelines as a small newspaper foundered on the Northern Ireland issue in the early 1970s. The paper was set up as a genuinely alternative newspaper, that would seek out alternative viewpoints on subjects where there appeared to be an establishment consensus in the national press. Violence was on the increase in Northern Ireland and the paper faced the issue squarely in accordance with its stated policy, reporting not so much on the violence of the opposing and bloody-minded factions in the province, as on the violence of the methods used by the army in dealing with these factions. And, as has subsequently been officially admitted, certain methods used by the army at that time were far from blameless. But having apparently taken sides through its alternative report-ing, the newspaper began attracting into its offices people who fed the newspaper with inaccurate information and expected the newspaper to ally itself to their causes irrespective of the realities. There were disagreements within the staff on edi-torial policy. The Northern Ireland coverage lost those readers looking for a comfortably London-oriented extension of the underground press. The paper ran into financial troubles. And closed. It would be possible to blame the closure on ill-formed policy at the outset, inflexibility in style and format, staff troubles, not enough money; but I believe the attempt to be radical in the face of the Northern Ireland nightmare killed that paper.

How then does adult education, feeling its way towards community control, deal with the possibility that someone might want a course on the IRA's viewpoint in Northern Ireland? Of course we can duck the issue immediately. The IRA is a proscribed organisation and we do not have to have anything to do with anyone who might be connected with it. Or we could wrap ourselves around with that special brand of antiseptic cotton wool used by the other sectors of the educa-tion service, and respond with a conventional course consisting of a series of detached and analytical lectures by an academic with expertise in the fields of history and the political and social sciences. Perhaps this is the wisest, and only, way we could do it. But it leaves me dissatisfied, and aware that the students of such a course would depart with their knowledge of the subject drawn from second-hand sources. After all, what do we know about the IRA? Our information comes from journals and newspapers and is all second-hand. These reports present a very nasty picture, but just conceivably there is another side to the story that we, living across the water and out of earshot of the cries of agony of the victims and the screams of rage of the murderers, have simply never heard. Would it not be illuminating, in a very terrible way, to meet and discuss with people who advocate the use of the sort of violence that is at present part of Ulster's daily life? Would this not be a valid way of trying to understand the incomprehensible? Would this not be a valid way of trying to understand the conditions of the province—the years of inequality, bigotry, electoral engineering, poverty, powerlessness and misuse of power—that have produced people on both sides who in appearance remain human and yet are capable of such inhuman acts? Would there not be a value in hearing and being able to discuss and contest (and contest and contest again) the story from the horse's mouth?

In asking questions like these of a service whose major concern is the provision of tuition in hobbies and interests I may appear to be straying too ridiculously far into the funny-land of the hypothetical. But are these questions as meaningless and hopelessly hypothetical when related to another group of people who, far from being proscribed, constitute a political party and in their public pronouncements and the management of their affairs remain within the law? Are there any educational justifications, along the lines of those discussed in relation to the Northern Ireland extremists, for an adult education centre to provide a platform for the National Front?

Political Responsibility

Throughout this book I have emphasised the adult educator's responsibility to the community. I have argued that adult education is based on response to demand and that a centre is woven by as many strands as there are students into the fabric of the communities in the area it serves. But the adult educator has responsibilities in another direction. He has political masters, and he must answer to them as well.

Often people seem to assume that the education service is somehow outside politics. A vague parallel is drawn with the judiciary. Both education and the judiciary are seen to be dealing with absolutes — truth, justice — and are therefore not subject to politically motivated control. But this is nonsense.[34] The education service is tied into the political structure of the country and controlled by politicians. Indeed education is a major political football, with politicians of all levels from local councillors to the Prime Minister ready to do battle over it. Much is made of education's duty to produce independent-minded, creative, self-fulfilled people; but it is also clear that those in power or those striving for power see the education service as an instrument for wielding massive long-term political influence. Those in power see it as an arm of the state whose purpose is to prepare people to fit into an existing system and provide the workforce and brainpower for the country's economy. (Again and again, for example, in the so-called Great Debate on education in 1977 the politicians and industry returned to the question of standards in mathematics and the sciences, arguing that it was proficiency in these areas that in our present technological age made people productive participants in the economic life of the country.) Those striving for change, on the other hand, want to use the education service as a means of propagating their ideas and of preparing people to play a part in the new order. Whatever his political hue, no politician is going to ignore education. Rather he is going to take every opportunity to bring it into line with his political vision, and do his best to keep the opposition's hands off it.

Because the education service is subject to political control it is inevitable that from time to time, whether we like it or not, decisions will be taken in educational matters for reasons of political expediency or policy. This political control can hamper educational adventure, and where it does the adult educator must express his disagreement as forcefully as possible, but it can also provide a check. It can, to be ingloriously frank, take the adult educator off the hook. It is extremely unlikely that any local authority would permit one of its adult education centres to run a course on and by the National Front. I could mount an educational argument against such a course, but I would be using words such as 'integrity' and 'wisdom' and 'quality' and I doubt whether the politicians would have much time for this sort of talk. Indeed I doubt whether they would consider the educational arguments at all. All they would be intent on doing would be to prevent that particular part of the opposition from gaining a foothold in one of their services, and the major part of the opposition from gaining a brickbat with which to beat them over the head. The majority party would exercise their right as the elected masters of the adult educator to veto the course.

And because I have political opinions too, I would applaud this use of their power. My only worry would be that they would accompany their actions with a lot of loose talk about educational theory and practice, rather than frankly admit that their decision was a political one.

Chapter 25

Community

The worry about whom the adult educator should approach or willingly respond to, the worry about priorities in the allocation of a centre's resources, is exacerbated and may even be caused by the continual confusion over the word 'community'. Adult education is being urged to increase its community provision, to cater more meaningfully for the community, to orient itself more realistically towards community needs, but who are we actually referring to when we use this imprecise, foggy word?

Here are six reasonably common ways in which adult educators interpret the concept of 'community':

Community Equals the Working Class
Often when adult educators use the word 'community' they are actually referring to the working class. 'We must establish closer links with the community' means 'we must get more working-class people into our classes'. 'Community education' means in effect more provision of activities on a working-class estate. 'Making adult education more representative of community values' means reducing the number of activities attended by the middle classes or that promote middle-class culture, and increasing the number of activities that promote working-class culture.

Some adult educators arrive at this equation of community with the working class simply because they realise that one of their branches in a working-class area is patronised almost completely by middle-class commuters or because they have noted that only a small number of working-class people make use of their facilities overall. Without going into the matter too deeply they feel that any extra effort should be directed to attracting more working-class people into their activities in order to achieve a more realistic social mix. And they take practical steps to do just that, redesigning their publicity, reallocating classes to other branches, directing their outreach work towards recognisably working-class areas. They make no radical changes in their programme but simply seek to make the existing provision more accessible and tell more people about it.

Others make the equation of community with the working class because they see the working class consistently losing out both culturally and economically in a society controlled by middle-class institutions purveying middle-class values. These adult educators seek to reform their own institutions as a first step towards a more equitable education service. Frank Youngman, in *Planning Local Adult Education Provision*,[35] ends a section on establishing priorities with this uncompromising statement:

> The central problem remains that the Adult Education Service should offer recurrent educational opportunities to the majority of the nation that is failed by schools, yet it tends to attract only the minority who succeeded at school. I think the policies of Frobisher [Adult Education Institute] should be measured according to the success with which its service is made accessible or responsive to the working-class people within its area.

Others make the equation because of an unequivocal political commitment to the working class. They see adult education as a potential agent for raising working-class consciousness, an agency through which an attack on the maldistribution of educational, social and economic opportunities can begin to be mounted. They see adult education as an agent for social change. Keith Jackson, for example, interprets community development in terms of the conflict of class interests. In an article entitled 'The Marginality of Community Development —Implications for Adult Education'[36] he warns against the concept of community development as a process to integrate communities 'into the life of the nation'. He goes on:

But this is politics, and why not say so? 'Neutral' community development workers are government agents at the local level. In industrial society this could only mean that the so-called 'communities' — usually in working-class areas — are to be integrated into the life of the ruling class, or elites.

To counter this he directs his attention to 'working-class activists', reaching this conclusion:

Evidence suggests that the alienation of working-class students from education results from their recognition that it does not reflect their values, and is not useful in pursuing their collective interests. Educationalists must therefore enter into a dialogue with working-class activists and 'students', from a position of solidarity with them, so that they may interpret their social situation, and the actions they take, in the light of their own values and interests.

And in summary he identifies three basic concerns for the adult educator involved in 'local social action':

Marginal reform of educational practices, a broader interpretation of significant resources, and a recognition of the need for economic strategies such as positive discrimination.

Political and social organisation involving co-option and alliances; both to release further resources and to shift power through changing relations with working-class activists, leading perhaps to more substantial reform.

Intervention to increase consciousness and awareness of social realities and of actions which are being taken, to alter these realities, leading perhaps to radical reform which cannot be contained within existing institutions.

Tom Lovett is equally clear about where his primary concern lies in his book *Adult Education, Community Development and the Working Class*[37], and he is among the most outspoken critics of adult education's failure to cater for the working class:

The adult education movement in this country has never successfully tackled the problem of education for working-class communities. This is particularly true of that section of the working class to be found in EPAs (educational priority areas)—unskilled and semi-skilled workers suffering from a wide range of economic, social and educational deprivation. Certainly, the WEA and some of the university extra-mural departments have in recent years greatly extended their work with the trade union movement—mainly courses of a vocational nature for shop stewards—but it is generally accepted that those attending these classes are something of an elite amongst the working class. In fact, it is extremely doubtful if the adult education movement *ever* attracted students from the lower working class.[38]

There are still others who make the equation of community with the working class, not necessarily because of a sense of political solidarity with the working class, but because they see adult education as having a particular cultural mission to perform. These adult educators will argue that adult education is in part a guardian of our heritage; that with the passing of the village artisan, adult education now has an important role to play in keeping alive and passing on traditional skills and crafts. And they will argue that since middle-class culture is enshrined in most of our institutions, it is the duty of adult education to counter-balance this and orient a significant amount of its provision to maintaining and promoting working-class culture.

This commitment to getting the working class in or promoting specifically working-class activities can lead to an inverted snobbery. The new guard are particularly prone to this. Working-class becomes best and 'middle-class' a pejorative term. 'But did any real people come?' a community worker will ask of a meeting. Somehow the belief is fostered that to be working-class is to be more genuine, gutsier, straighter; and as a result of this prejudice certain subjects will become identified as middle-class activities and judged not worth supporting. Poor old badminton is one of these and so, ridiculously enough, is pottery.

Certainly there should be a reaction against the middle-class monopoly of adult education — and there seems to be a general consensus that this is the case — but it should not take the form of an over-reaction in which the middle classes are automatically found wanting, and so-called middle-class subjects sent packing. 1977 saw the providers of community education in Coventry considering a plan to concentrate their provision in a working-class sector of the city and to make traditional adult education provision elsewhere in the city more financially self-supporting. But there are dangers in such a concentration of resources. The adult education service may very quickly lose its comprehensive character and the flexibility of response that goes with it. Dismiss middle-class support and the poor cousin may become even more marginal than it is at present. Dismiss middle-class support and a centre may lose its base of traditional provision from which it can reach out and engage in community development and action.[39]

Community Equals Quiescent Poor
Working-class people may not be satisfied in adult education terms with the provision of classes in pigeon fancying and dressmaking on a low budget. In an area where most of the wage earners work for one large employer the demand might just as easily be for a course on employment rights or Marxism or the politics and legalities of industrial action.

These harsh possibilities cause some adult educators, consciously or unconsciously, to shy away from the equation of community with the working class and limit themselves in their community work to the provision of 'non-controversial' activities such as keep-fit or arts and crafts classes in areas where people are poor and living in poor housing conditions. 'Community' in their terms now means 'quiescent poor only'.

The fact that some adult educators do make this equation was brought home to me in a discussion I had with two senior colleagues and my principal about the special studies courses at Addison. One of them had expressed reservations about some of our methods and my principal, perhaps to demonstrate to my critic that I was not all mad or totally bad, mentioned that I also went to a factory two mornings a week before the morning shift to teach English to a group of Asian women working there. My critic looked at me and said with very real feeling: 'Now that's what you *should* be doing!'

But this sort of attitude can imply an excessive paternalism. There is a danger of a throwback to the thinking of some Victorian good-works charity in which middle-class education is doled out to the working classes as long as they knuckle under. This may seem far-fetched when stated so baldly, but I detect something of this attitude in the way many of the new guard refer to working-class women. Spurred on by the pre-school playgroups movement and examples such as the Allfarthing family workshop, many adult educators have made very real efforts to provide activities for the parents of small children — arts and crafts groups, mothers and toddlers clubs, demonstration cookery classes with a makeshift crèche attached, and so on. The people responsible for this sort of provision have every right to be proud of it, but some seem to consider it the be-all and end-all of community education; and too many refer to the women making use of this sort of provision as 'working-class mums'.

The word 'mum' is a demeaning word, implying warmth and emotion but no imagination or thought. It deprives the person referred to of her individuality, turning her into a homely stereotype. When I hear adult educators referring to their 'working-class mums' I have a feeling that they are implying that the women are manipulable, and are taking comfort from their powerlessness.

Community Equals the Disadvantaged

Some adult educators see all their community work in terms of providing for the disadvantaged. The term 'disadvantaged' came into vogue in the early seventies replacing such terms as 'needy', 'underprivileged' and 'deprived', and was enshrined in a major recommendation in the *Russell Report* that 'more positive effort should be directed towards the disadvantaged' (page x, para. 3.6). But from the very beginning of its use in the adult education context the term was too broad to have any really useful meaning. Peter Clyne in his research for the Russell Committee, subsequently published in his book *The Disadvantaged Adult*, lists nine categories of people who can be regarded as disadvantaged:

Adult illiterates
Those in need of remedial education
Mentally ill
Mentally handicapped
Physically handicapped
Non-English-speaking immigrants
Deaf and hard of hearing
Blind and partially sighted
Elderly

— thus apparently lumping together in the same category an Indian immigrant whose only disability is his lack of fluent English, an Englishman confined to a wheelchair as a result of a car accident, and an adult who has been severely mentally handicapped since birth.

And from this very broad start, as the word has been used in policy statements, memoranda and reports, so its terms of reference have broadened. The *Russell Report* swept into the net 'the physically and mentally handicapped as well as those who, on account of their limited educational background, present cultural or social environment, age, location, occupation or status, cannot easily take part in adult education as normally provided' (para. 277). An ILEA circular added to the list 'those in hospitals, homes, prisons, etc., and other welfare groups; and the lonely and the shy'.[40] The 1976 ILEA report 493 added parents of handicapped children and women at maternity and child welfare centres . . . and so on, although the word had already attained its apotheosis of meaningless for me at a meeting about outreach work in late 1974 when this remark was made: 'But we are all disadvantaged in some way, aren't we?'

This over-use of the word would be laughable if it did not seriously mislead as well. Even Peter Clyne's list of nine categories[41] confuses the issue in that it blurs the distinction between people who, given access to the right kind of support, can help themselves, and those who, because of the kind or degree of their disability, are unable to help themselves. Adult education is subject to control by the users and is an experience in sharing among adults as equals. In any adult education activity, in effect, there is a large element of self-help. In the case of many of the groups listed under the blanket term of 'the disadvantaged' — the physically handicapped, the blind, the deaf, the socially deprived — such basic conditions can obtain. Some of the groups and some of the individuals within the groups will need intensive support, including special facilities, but they can still exert control over the educational provision they take part in. But there are some groups, or members of some groups, who through the severity of their disability are unable to exert control over the provision. In the case of the severely mentally ill, the severely mentally handicapped, some of the very elderly, the provision will have to be so specialised and so completely organised by the professional that it ceases to have much common ground with the rest of adult education.[42]

That is not to say that adult education should wash its hands of these groups. Adult education should seek to play a part in the educational activities of all groups within the community, but institutionalised and non-institutionalised groups should not be included in the same broad category. That might not matter if the lumping together of the institutionalised with the non-institutionalised meant that the adult educator then adopted non-institutionalised attitudes to everyone. But unfortunately the reverse tends to happen. The adult educator is led very easily into adopting a paternalistic, even authoritarian, approach to *all* groups he has denoted as disadvantaged.

The very word 'disadvantaged' helps compound this paternalistic approach. It suggests a lack, an emptiness, in the people so described which we, the purveyors of education with our 'body of knowledge', must set about filling. But many of the groups described as disadvantaged have a body of knowledge and a culture of their own. The elderly have a personal experience of the past that we younger people working with them only know at second hand. The blind have their own organisations, means of communication and body of expertise — in relation to the complex techniques of blind mobility, for example. And certain groups described as 'socially deprived' use a form of the language, adopt a life-style and interrelate in ways that mark them off from other sections of the community in a clear and positive way. Rather than being the empty vessels that the adult educator must rush to fill with his particular (usually middle-class) culture, many of the groups that are labelled 'disadvantaged' have a body of knowledge and culture to communicate or build upon themselves. If the adult educator is to provide something educationally valid, he must learn about this body of knowledge and become acquainted with the group's own culture first, and work from there.[43]

Because some of the groups under the disadvantage label are institutionalised and isolated from the rest of the community, the temptation is to consider the other groups as isolated by their particular disability too. Provision for the physically handicapped becomes a limited programme of arts and crafts classes at a local government lunch club. By providing for each group of the disadvantaged on their own institutional premises, the adult educator can avoid the arduous task of reordering his thinking and the facilities of his centre so that individuals suffering from particular disabilities can join in its general provision alongside non-disadvantaged members of the community. He can very easily fall into the trap of locating the blame for a group's non-use of his centre in that group's particular disability, rather than taking a long hard look at himself and his centre to see whether the reason for the group's non-use might be closer to home. The 'socially deprived' may stay away in their droves, not because that is the way with the socially deprived, but because of the centre's smugly superior atmosphere. The physically handicapped may stay away in their droves because the centre has never devised an uncomplicated and unembarrassing method of reception. And the elderly may stay away in their droves not just because they are elderly but because the authorities have chosen to locate daytime adult education facilities in that area (as they have at Addison) on the top floor of a building that has no lift!

Community Equals 'the Whole Community'

And then there is the 'whole community' brigade. Working together with the other sectors of the education service, they say, adult education should seek to provide an education service for the whole community. 'The whole community' is a seductive phrase, seemingly including every single one of us and broadly hinting at the deschoolers' idea of the community as one large organic learning unit. But this, of course, would require a complete revolution in educational thinking, so not surprisingly the phrase usually implies something rather more modest.

So modest, in fact, that many of the projects that come under the banner of an education service for the whole community turn out, once the verbiage of the accompanying literature is stripped away, to be unadventurous exercises in parent education. Parent education varies from attempts to involve parents in the day-to-day running of their children's school, to a formal series of lectures under some such title as 'Your Child at Primary School', to parents coming to the school in the evening to experience the classroom activities their children engage in during the day. This involvement is valuable for the school and the few parents who do take part, but as a move towards an education service for the whole community it must be recognised as little more than tokenism. If we were to take parent education seriously, if we were seriously to recognise the extent to which a child's education is influenced by parental attitudes at home, then rather than setting up the occasional school-linked evening class we should be throwing major resources into equipping parents to play a full educational role in bringing up their children. We should be radically re-educating adults. We should be shifting resources from school education into adult education. This would involve a comprehensive system of day-release from work for working parents, grants, subsidies . . .[44] But we are back to the idea of a revolution in our educational system — an all-out attempt to involve the whole community rather than the token classes on a couple of evenings a week for parents highly motivated enough to attend and not too tired after a full day's work.

Even when the advocates of an education service for the whole community look beyond parental involvement they are rarely talking about creating a recurrent education service literally available to everyone. More often the adult educator using the phrase is talking about achieving a mix of students in his centre that is representative of the population of his area. He may strive for a more accurate reflection of the social classes, or age groupings. Or a more even balance of the sexes. Or a representative number of people from ethnic minorities.

Instead of conceiving of the community as a complex whole, he is more likely to think of the community in terms of a number of separate, clearly definable categories; and then judge his success in catering for 'the whole community' by the extent to which he manages to draw in a roughly proportional representation from each of these categories.

Community Equals Acceptable Community

Often the categories selected by the adult educator do not take in anything like the whole community. It is unusual for an adult educator to consider it part of his task to cater for dossers, or business people, or the unemployed, or homosexuals, for example. The idea of the whole community has certain understood limits, and nowhere is this more forcefully demonstrated than on the cover of an ILEA report, *An Education Service for the Whole Community* (1973). With such a title one would expect the cover to carry one of those staged photographs showing fifty or so people grouped together in the middle of a street all smiling up at the camera. They would be all ages, sizes and races. Some would look conventional and some extravagant and unconventional. There would be a city gent, a young drop-out, a policewoman, an office worker, a rasta, someone holding a football. In the background there might be some shops, a factory, a pub, houses, a field with a tractor in it, and so on and so on . . . But no, the cover actually carries a photograph of a white, well-dressed, middle-class family standing outside a modern school building. The youngest, a boy of about twelve, is holding a book open and the others are admiring the work he has done in the building behind them. There are thirteen other people in the background, all of them white and equally middle-class in appearance. Considering that the report states that 19.95 per cent of the resident population of the ILEA area in 1971 were born outside the UK, for the photographer to have found such an exclusively English group of people coming out of an ILEA school must be rated a notable achievement. In fact the report does recognise that ILEA's future provision 'must be based on the existence of a multi-racial society' (para. 11) but in all other respects the cover of the report sets the tone for what is inside. The community is seen in conventional terms, with the education service remaining institution-based. While arguing for an increased and interrelated use of existing institutions, an extension of resources to cater for certain sectors of society felt to be missed by current provision, and an increase in parent involvement and parent education, the report offers nothing to meet the radical promise of its title.

Community Equals Society

And so to a use of the word 'community' that contains no idea of community at all. Sometimes when using the word the adult educator is using it in the same way as a judge or a politician or a headmaster might use the word 'society'.

'Society requires that you be incarcerated for the remainder of your natural life.'

'Society requires laws and lawmakers.'

'Society rewards hard work.'

In the word 'society' there can reside a ringing, unquestionable authority. It suggests all the force of consensus opinion. The speaker will often be a person in authority himself who by virtue of his position claims the right to speak for the rest of us. And yet when we look at the pronouncements they often turn out to be based on assumptions and very little else. The judge who invokes society may in fact be expressing nothing more than a personal assessment, based perhaps on years of personal experience, but not less personal for that. He bases his judgement on what he 'knows' of society, although that knowledge may be limited to the artificial world of the courtroom and, outside that, his own class, age group, and personal circle. And even if the speaker is wise beyond the wisest judge or politician or headmaster, any appeal to the authority of society is based upon the further dubious assumption that society is a homogeneous whole that can be represented in clear, unequivocal statements without any great difficulty.

The community can be appealed to in the same way by an adult educator looking for an authority for his actions or policy.

'The community is not yet ready for such a course.'

'In any question of priorities, the community must come first.'

Ringing phrases but as unverifiable, as empty pieces of rhetoric, as an appeal to society. Indeed you could exchange 'the community' for 'society' without any great change in the meaning (or meaninglessness) of the phrases.

Multiplicity of Interests

There is probably no single, satisfactory definition of 'community'. But we mistinterpret the word grossly if we appeal to the community as any kind of incontrovertible authority, or if we assume that the community can be represented by a single voice. One of the clues to the meaning of 'community' lies in its utter *lack* of any statutory authority.

'The community needs a new sports centre.'

The community may indeed need a new sports centre, but so what? The need may be screamingly obvious and there may be any number of local people and community organisations agitating for an increase in sporting facilities, but in the statement there is no hint of any external pressure such as a law or government or the education system obliging anyone actually to build the centre.

And although the word 'community' can be used apparently to encompass everyone, the concept does not imply a majority of people thinking, believing and behaving in unison. Rather it implies a multiplicity of interests. When not used synonymously with 'society', the word 'community' usually refers to minorities—lots of them bundled together and intersecting and interrelating in a myriad ways but minorities nevertheless. And if the adult educator uses the word 'community' correctly, I believe he is indicating his willingness to listen to, learn from and respond to minorities.

One Step Forward and Two Steps Sideways...

ILEA has demonstrated how difficult it is to decide on priorities in the way it has veered over the last seven or eight years from one interpretation of community education to another. A working party was set up in 1970 to investigate the reasons for the low enrolment of unskilled and semi-skilled workers in ILEA adult education institutes. The starting-point, therefore, was quite clearly a concern with the need to increase the provision for the working class. But the working party went beyond its terms of reference and when it reported in 1973 made its recommendations in terms of institutes responding to the educational needs of the 'wider community', saying this in its conclusions:

> We believe that if the basic approach is right, then adult education should naturally attract and serve a complete cross-section of the community without any need for special discriminatory measures between arbitrarily defined sectors.[45]

Out goes the unequivocal concern for the working class and in comes the concept of serving 'a complete cross-section of the community'. This 'whole community' approach was reinforced by the report *An Education Service for the Whole Community* published later that same year. In the meantime, however, the *Russell Report* had been published advocating that a more positive effort be directed towards the disadvantaged. Naturally this influenced ILEA thinking, and the onset of financial hard times reinforced this redirection towards the disadvantaged. Back came the policy of positive discrimination (although now in favour of the disadvantaged rather than the unskilled or semi-skilled worker) to ride in uncomfortable tandem with the policy of provision for the whole community.

But, as we have seen, the concept of 'the disadvantaged' has its drawbacks and confusions too, so that by 1976 ILEA memoranda and discussion documents were beginning to use the phrase 'special community needs', which can mean a lot or remarkably little, depending on the user's decision as to what is or is not sufficiently special. The list of people with 'special community needs' that appears in ILEA report 493, which was circulated to institutes for discussion in 1977, is made up of the groups we have become accustomed to seeing listed under the heading of 'the disadvantaged' but now it has the appearance of an arbitrarily selected set of categories to which I might want to add my own nominations and from which someone else might want to remove his. The concept of 'special community need' begins to look like an escape clause. What is more, if one removes the word 'community' from the phrase the meaning is unchanged. People in prison and 'stroke' patients are described as people with 'special community needs' but they could equally well be described as people with 'special needs', leading one to suspect that the word 'community' is left in as a hangover from the past, and possibly abandoned, policies. Certainly the 493 report and an accompanying one numbered 770, both discussion documents concerned with future ILEA adult education policy, seem to have lost interest in adult education's potential role in aiding community development and action. One step forward, two steps sideways.

Positive Discrimination
In the debate about priorities the concern often seems to centre on the potential students rather than the activities they might engage in. The talk is about groups and categories and socio-economic classes that adult education is failing to reach and rarely about the subject-matter or character of the activities we might provide for all these people we are failing to reach. The assumption seems to be that what adult education can provide is essentially uniform and non-controversial. But this is simply not the case. Adult education can offer an almost limitless variety of activities, some of them leisure learning, others survival learning, some non-controversial, others one-sided and political in intent; and any discussion of priorities must consider what sort of activities to provide as well as who we are providing them for.

Take the case of an adult education centre pursuing a policy of positive discrimination in favour of the disadvantaged. There are two ways of doing this. The soft option would be for the centre to increase its provision of welfare classes and be done with that. Welfare classes are activities run in conjunction with the local statutory and voluntary agencies and for the most part take place on those agencies' premises. Thus a soft option method of providing for the physically handicapped would be to increase the number of music and movement and craft activities the centre supports at the local government day centre for the handicapped. This is all very well, assuming of course that the physically handicapped at the centre actually wanted an increase in these activities. But it would still leave the physically handicapped isolated at the day centre engaged in activities whose main function was to prevent them going mad with boredom or passing away as a result of physical inactivity. While the adult educator fulfils an important role by providing these kinds of activity, he must remember that in themselves the activities are only minimally educational. They do not constitute an increase in the educational opportunities for the physically handicapped, nor do they investigate why the rest of society treats the physically handicapped with such disdain and consistently fails to design buildings, transport and everyday amenities with them in mind. The soft option form of positive discrimination rarely moves towards change. It involves little action and is often really only an extension of the social services.

The hard option, on the other hand, involves the commitment and intensity of involvement that that outreach worker gave to those dossers. Here the adult educator is not concerned with stopping gaps in the social services and filling in people's time. He is concerned with examining problems and investigating ways of putting them right. That outreach worker did not enter that day centre with the intention of limiting his response to leisure learning activities only. He did not intend to set up a course in billiards and so improve the dossers' standards of play. Rather he came to talk to the dossers, to listen to them, to see whether they could answer the question of why they were dossers in the first place, and to see whether they might want to consider doing anything to change their situation. The adult educator who chooses the hard option recognises that while there are groups of people who can be categorised as disadvantaged, then society is manifestly unfair. And he devotes a good part of his energies, and reallocates a good part of his resources, to providing activities that will point this out, search for reasons, postulate answers, and encourage change.

Availability
What then is the answer? How do adult educators decide which groups or categories or social classes they should approach or angle their programme at? How do they decide which courses to put on? With so many potential demands on their limited resources, how do they decide on priorities?

There is no complete answer to this. Obviously with communities varying enormously from one part of the country to another, so will their requirements and so will adult education's response. There is simply no way in which we could arrive at some recommended division of resources that would be applicable to all areas and all communities. And it would be counter to everything argued in this book even to try.

But there is a part answer and it lies in the centre adopting a policy of availability. Since they cannot positively discriminate in favour of everyone, adult educators will have to make choices. Instead of striving after some artificial balance in their programme, or attempting to part-satisfy everyone, they should make their choices boldly. Obviously they will have to make them with due reference to their masters' policy decisions and the demands of their students and the people in their area, but they should go for the groups and causes they believe in. If it be the mentally handicapped, so be it. If they see the growing problem of unemployment as being more important, so be it. In other words, they should positively discriminate as they think fit. But discrimination in favour of one group or category is only justifiable if resources are held available for others. And not only those who have the knowledge and persistence to wrest them from the centre. Adult educators must take positive action to make their resources *readily* available. They must look for opportunities to demonstrate their centre's availability. And they must make themselves accessible. They must be in constant contact with people in their area. Their choice of priorities may not please everyone, and they should be available to explain their choice, receive criticism and respond to counter demands.

I have earlier expressed the dual responsibilities of adult educators in terms of their 'active' and 'passive' relationship to their communities. Here I want to rephrase the idea and say that the policy of positive discrimination should be accompanied by a clearly formulated policy of positive availability.

Chapter 26

The Crunch

Participatory Versus Elective Democracy

Adult education is based in principle on participatory democracy. A large web of pressure groups exert their control
through the continual expression of demand, even if that
demand is simply that a dressmaking class continue for
another year and is expressed by virtue of the fact that the
group continued attending throughout the previous year. In
fact control in adult education can, and to a large extent does,
come from the bottom up rather than the top down. But the
central bureaucracy, of which the adult education agency is a
part, is subject to the traditional forms of bureaucratic control
in which officers try to reflect the policy of elected representatives and in which control comes from the top down via a fairly
rigid hierarchy.

The crunch comes when a genuine community demand runs
counter to centralised majority policy.

No Sex Please, We're ILEA

In July 1973 the South London Gay Liberation Front decided
to approach ILEA with a view to setting up a 'Gay Studies'
course. They formed an education group to prepare a syllabus
and co-ordinate the recruitment of speakers. These were the
subjects the group decided on:

1 Sexism and the family: the psychology of sex role learning in
   the human male and female.
2 The psychology of human relationships, or sex and love and
   other aspects of being human.

3 The sociology of homosexuality in Britain; or where, who and what are gay people in this country.
4 Medical aspects of physical relationships in sex.
5 The politics of gay liberation; the place of gay men and women in modern society.
6 Communal living: a study of possible future life-styles.

The group then approached an ILEA recreational institute in South London, which put the idea up to the central authority. After a little toing and froing of letters, ILEA invited the South London GLF education group to a meeting with the principal of the institute and two ILEA officers at County Hall on 9 October 1973. Two GLF members — a psychologist and a further education lecturer — went to put their case and after a lengthy discussion were told that ILEA would not support the course.

The chairman of the South London GLF education group wrote a report of the meeting, giving his version of the reasons put forward by the officers for the refusal of the course. But the refusal alone poses important questions of principle. Here was an education authority rejecting a demand for educational support from a group legally within the community. Was ILEA refusing to accept the challenge and do its job? Was ILEA making a moral rather than an educational judgement? Was ILEA making false assumptions about the people who would attend the course? Was ILEA unaware of the extent of public interest in the subject? (After all, there had been a debate in Parliament culminating in the 1967 change in the legislation on homosexuality; there had been a recent increase in the number of organisations campaigning for homosexual rights; and what figures there were suggested that a not inconsiderable number of people had direct experience of homosexuality. [46]) In short, was ILEA acting out of ignorance and prejudice? The *South London Press* suspected as much and in a leading article on 30 October said that ILEA seemed 'to have joined ranks with the intolerant'.

On the face of it ILEA's refusal stood as a sobering example of how it was all right to go along with a community education policy just so far. This point was not missed by the chairman of the South London GLF education group, who noted in his report that, on the same day as his meeting with the ILEA officers, the ILEA education committee had met to discuss the Education Officer's new report entitled *An Education Service for the Whole Community*. And the public pronouncements by the chairman of ILEA's further and higher education sub-committee in response to press comment certainly lent strength to the suspicion that the refusal was the result of defensive thinking rather than any clearly formulated policy. On 2 November in *The Times Educational Supplement* the chairman was quoted as saying:

> Nothing we have done in any sense prevents the Gay Liberation movement from running its own course. The issue is simply whether this authority should spend money on providing such a course which could be equally provided by the Gay Liberation Front themselves.

This is the classic we-have-done-nothing riposte, and it will not hold up. The South London GLF applied because they wanted the support, the facilities, and the advice with which to run a better course than they could themselves. They wanted to establish a dialogue. This is how the chairman of the South London GLF education group expressed it in his report:

> The course was to be aimed at the general public, both gay and straight, a particular welcome being extended to those, who, by virtue of their work, either come into contact with gay people, or are in a position to disseminate more widely the information and ideas necessary for the promotion of greater public understanding of homosexuality — for example, teachers, social workers, members of the medical and legal professions, the police and the youth services.

It is unlikely that many representatives from these professional groups would have attended a course run by the GLF and no one else, since some at least would have been reluctant to enter the gay pub or gay centre where the privately sponsored course was being held and so risk being identified personally with the gay cause. But with the course held under the auspices of an education authority in a school building and alongside any number of other educational activities, the story might have been very different. People interested in, but not necessarily associated with or even sympathetic to the cause of homosexual liberation would feel less inhibited about attending. On this 'neutral' ground everyone involved would be much more likely to engage in the dialogue the GLF wanted.

Furthermore, if ILEA's policy were really to be found in the statement by the chairman of the further and higher education sub-committee, then what justification had Addison for sponsoring the Red Cross Over Sixty Club's crafts and singing sessions? Perhaps we should say: 'These courses could equally be provided by the Over Sixty Club themselves', and withdraw our support. If adult education were to adopt the we-have-done-nothing line of reasoning it would lose all credibility as a community service.

Gay Studies at Addison

When I heard that the South London GLF had been knocked back, I decided to try and set up much the same course myself, hoping that if the proposal came from within the service and were put forward in the context of Addison's special studies programme ILEA's response might be different.

My aim was to provide a course that would deal with homosexuality from the homosexual's point of view. This meant using speakers from the various organisations campaigning for homosexual rights or who were sympathetic to the concept of homosexual equality, and appointing a course co-ordinator whom these speakers would trust—in other words, basing the course design on the model we had developed in previous courses such as 'Black Experience', 'Alternative Societies', 'Civil Liberties'; and 'Women and Men'. And since the point of the course would be to investigate certain common assumptions about homosexuality, the last thing I wanted to do was to appoint a course co-ordinator whose particular professionalism would presuppose answers to some of the questions the course was meant to ask. I did not want a medical doctor in the chair, for example, since no matter what his personal views were, his appointment would tend to presuppose that homosexuality was an illness. Nor a criminologist, since this appointment might appear to confirm rather than critically examine the assertion that homosexuality was a deviance. In order to provide a course that would take these common assumptions apart, that would challenge majority beliefs, that would make people think, it seemed essential that the course co-ordinator should be extremely well-informed in the subject, a skilful chairman, a person of integrity—and a homosexual.

I talked the idea over with my principal and several colleagues, then early in 1974 met the chairman of the South London GLF education group. He was a stocky man, in his late twenties, with an open face on which one could easily read his determination and, when things went against his cause, his distress and hurt. Against his naturally retiring character he had forced himself into the public arena to fight against what he saw as the persecution of those who were openly homosexual and the oppression of those homosexuals who for any number of reasons had not 'come out'. I liked him immediately, and quickly felt I could trust him to chair the course. We discussed the project in detail and once we had decided to go ahead he invited me to speak at one of the regular Wednesday evening meetings of the South London GLF at their centre in Brixton. At that meeting I discussed with about twenty-five people the form the course should take, the kinds of speaker we should invite, and the tone to aim for. I mention the tone since in all my contacts with the GLF I was struck by their insistence that the course be conducted in a relaxed, open way, and that every precaution be taken to avoid its deteriorating into a sterile confrontation between opposing viewpoints.

On 9 April Addison sent the copy for its 1974-5 prospectus to County Hall for approval. Along with the descriptions of the other twenty-six special studies courses intended for the coming year was this one under the title of 'Homosexuality':

A look at the social, legal and emotional attitudes towards homosexuality. Psychology of sex role learning, psychology of human relationships, sociology of homosexuality, the politics of gay liberation, communal living as a possible future life-style. Speakers will include a sociologist, a psychologist and representatives from the Gay Liberation movement.

And at the same time I submitted the usual form listing the tutor's academic and teaching qualifications and including under the section asking for experience relevant to the course, details of his involvement in the gay liberation movement.

There followed a silence from County Hall extending beyond the copy deadline for Addison's prospectus. We sent the copy to the printer.

Then vague rumbles from the central authority began, but not just about the course on 'Homosexuality'. A course on astrology and a course called 'Women's Liberation' (a repeat of the 'Women and Men' course) drew comment as well. Doubts about the seriousness of the astrology course were dispelled in conversations with inspectors, but on 20 June an inspector wrote saying he was still talking to his colleagues about the 'more controversial' courses in our programme, and mentioning 'Homosexuality' and 'Women's Liberation'. He sought assurances from the principal that the courses would be approached with integrity and academic objectivity, and that they would not be sensational or propagandist. The principal replied, drawing attention to the fact that the courses would be taking place within the context of the special studies programme and arguing that what Addison was doing was 'serious, responsible and educationally valuable'. Addison was asked to change the description of the 'Women's Liberation' course from this:

A study . . . of the ways in which women are oppressed . . .

to this:

A study . . . of the ways in which women may be considered as disadvantaged . . .

And the authority fell silent again. We corrected the prospectus proofs and returned them to the printer. The presses rolled, and Addison's 1974-5 prospectus hit the streets carrying the news that in the autumn the institute would be running a six-meeting course on 'Homosexuality'.

Still No Sex, Please

On 8 August the authority wrote to the institute. However, since Addison was closed for the month it was not until the first Monday in September that the principal opened and read the letter. It was in two short paragraphs. The first referred to the GLF request for a course on 'Gay Studies'. The second paragraph noted the similarity of Addison's proposed course on 'Homosexuality', and refused to approve it.

The reason given for the refusal was that it was established ILEA practice not to favour sectarian groups with particular beliefs, attitudes or ways of life. This was an odd reason to give since even a cursory glance through the ILEA programme indicated that it was the authority's established practice to do exactly the opposite; that there were ILEA institutes providing support for Jewish and Islamic groups, Christians and Buddhists. But the letter referred to homosexuals and the GLF, indicating that its interpretation of the word 'sectarian' went wider than the religious one, which put its assertions even more at variance with the facts. What about the black studies courses several institutes had run? Or the dancing and art and language classes for immigrant groups aimed at keeping them in touch with the beliefs, attitudes and ways of life that made up the cultures of their countries of origin? Read in this way the letter appeared not only to run counter to what many institutes had been doing with increasing success over the previous three or four years, but actually to reverse the policy of positive discrimination, except in the form of the blandest provision aimed at the most conventional sectors of society.

The worry was that if the letter were allowed to take its place unchallenged in the County Hall files it might gradually become accepted as an expression of central authority policy. And not just concerning homosexuality. Almost any gathering of people with common aims and interests and reasonably common life-styles could be described as 'sectarian'. I thought the matter over for a couple of days, and decided to fight the decision.

Alarums and Excursions

On 4 September 1974 I wrote to the chairman of the ILEA further and higher education sub-committee, bypassing my principal and his superiors. I received a reply on 17 September suggesting I take the matter up with my principal and the institute's academic board. But since a course on the subject of homosexuality had already been refused twice at central authority level, there seemed little point in taking the whole matter back to local level. On 27 September I wrote to the *Guardian*. I delivered the letter to the newspaper by hand and that same afternoon the *Guardian* rang the ILEA press officer, who set about ringing senior ILEA officers and my principal, who invited me into his office for a frank exchange of views . . .

But having gone to some pains to let my seniors know that I had written the letter, the *Guardian* printed nothing. I wondered what the ILEA press office might have said to curb the newspaper's initial interest, and on 3 October I sent the *Guardian* a photocopy of the authority's letter of refusal. By this stage I was no longer sure whether I was acting out of concern for the educational issues or whether I was grubbing after publicity as the only compensation I could expect from the unhappy situation I had put myself in; but I pressed on, informing a number of colleagues both inside and outside the ILEA service of the authority's action. On 21 October eleven outreach workers wrote a letter to the chairman of the further and higher education sub-committee, saying that they would welcome a chance to discuss the issues raised by the rejection of the course. And on 22 October, under the headline THE LOST COURSE, the *Guardian* printed a sarcastic little story in its education section quoting the authority's letter of refusal in full.

Carpeted
As a result of the story questions were asked in the County Hall council chamber and, in a classic bureaucratic move, it was announced that a working party would be set up to consider the problems that might arise when 'controversial' courses were applied for. Another result was that I was summoned into County Hall to be carpeted.

On the eve of my interview, in the best Thurberesque tradition, I took to my bed with a high temperature, and in the morning felt far from well. I left home as late as possible and took a taxi but got caught in a traffic jam and was forced to dive into the Underground and make a final dash across Westminster Bridge on foot, arriving at the appointed room in County Hall with thirty seconds to spare. There followed a long, and, on my side, feverish, interview with two officers. One of them described my actions as 'unworthy' and I began talking. Rash, insubordinate, unwise in my choice of action, perhaps. Unworthy, no. Appoint people to reach out into the community, appoint people to experiment, then you are going to have to support them. Ask them to operate on educational terms, then you must also. Ask them to go through the task of defining their community, then you cannot make a unilateral redefinition simply in order to suit some comfortable central policy.

Towards the end of the morning the senior of the two officers formally read out two paragraphs from the staff code, but by this stage the mood was slightly more amiable and I hoped I had demonstrated that I cared about adult education and had not been motivated by a fatuous or malicious desire simply to stir up trouble. I went home to bed.

Meetings, Meetings, Meetings

The working party comprising two officers, two inspectors, four principals and four outreach workers (of which I was one) first met on 17 March 1975 and continued meeting for well over a year. In the fullness of time we produced a report on *The Educational Approach to Controversial Learning Situations* from which I quoted on pages 174 and 179. The working party met ten times.

Back at Addison we started the long haul of proposing the course again. In the previous year I had made the application via the principal to the central authority, but in the meantime ILEA institutes had been equipped with academic boards and governing bodies, so that for 1975-6 my special studies programme had to be put to these two bodies for approval. The academic board met, considered the proposal, and appointed a sub-committee to go into the matter in more detail.

The sub-committee, comprising a cookery tutor, a keep-fit tutor, myself and another full-time member of staff, with the vice-principal in the chair, met three times. We looked at the form of the course and the context in which it would take place, met the chairman of the South London GLF education group, and decided by a 3:1 majority that 'a course dealing with homosexuality was a subject for inclusion in the institute's educational programme'. We also decided that the principle of employing a course co-ordinator who was homosexual was appropriate to the course but (such is the British genius for compromise) that the chairman of the South London GLF education group was too closely identified with the two previous proposals to be asked to co-ordinate this one.

The sub-committee's recommendations were now taken back to a full meeting of the academic board at which the course and the issues it raised were discussed for over an hour. The academic board made some changes to the wording of the recommendations and passed them on to a meeting of the governing body, at which most of the issues were discussed again. The governors made further alterations to the sub-committee's recommendations, and agreed that the course should go on.

This is the course description they decreed should appear in our 1975 - 6 prospectus:

HOMOSEXUALITY: CHANGING ATTITUDES

The course is open to any adult but is designed to be of particular interest to community and social workers, doctors and psychiatrists, the police, probation officers, teachers, the clergy—anyone who in the course of his/her work comes into contact with homosexuality.

The aim is to allow for a flexibility in the course design so that the group that enrols can decide on the subject to be examined. The pool of speakers for the course will contain professionals willing to speak about and discuss topics such as the legal position, religious aspects, psychological viewpoints etc., relating to homosexuality, and will include practising homosexuals.

As a course description it is little more than a statement of who might come followed by an outline of the structure to be adopted. But a bowdlerised result was hardly surprising since it did take three committees six meetings to write it.

The Course Co-ordinator

The governing body also decreed that the course co-ordinator must be a person 'of high academic standing, with special knowledge and an understanding of the position of the homosexual in society'. Although it had not been said in so many words I realised that it would be unwise to approach anyone else associated with the GLF, so I wrote to the Campaign for Homosexual Equality. An office-bearer replied, tentatively agreeing to co-ordinate the course. But we had to meet to be sure, and the meeting had to be very soon in order to beat my prospectus deadlines. He was based in the north and extremely busy, but was moving south for the next academic year; and I arranged to see him during the hour he would spend in London between trains on the way back from a house-hunting trip in the south. There was a fine irony in all this. I had spent a considerable amount of time getting to know the chairman of the GLF group, but was not permitted to employ him. Now, as a result of the delay caused by everyone's concern that we safeguard the educational standards of the course, here I was obliged to decide whether this man was suitable or not in the time it takes to drink a cup of tea in the Euston station self-service cafeteria.

But he *was* suitable, and the more I got to know him the more I realised how lucky I was that he had agreed to take the course on. He was a large man with sharp eyes and a dry wit. He had a first class arts degree, a postgraduate teaching qualification and a diploma in social work, and he had taught for several years in higher education. He was in his thirties, wore his hair cut short and was neatly conventional in his dress. He quickly understood what had been going on at County Hall, the constraints under which he would be working, and the kinds of misapprehension he might have to contend with. And he was, as *Gay News* described him, and as was to prove necessary during the course itself, unflappable.

I went back to the institute and put the course description into the page proofs of the prospectus; and a few weeks later went on my summer holidays, having spent the best part of an academic year over a proposed course of six meetings.

Anxieties

When I got back in September I was unable to contact the course co-ordinator. I had no telephone number and when I wrote to his new address I received no reply. With less than a month to go, and with people beginning to ask for details of the course, I was not even sure if I still had a course to offer.

The course co-ordinator did reply in time. He was going through the normal nightmarish delays in his house purchase and was still living in some grim lodging-house while mail addressed to his new address tended to go astray. Yes, he had begun to line up speakers. Yes, he was still going to take the course. Yes, he realised that I would be in a somewhat delicate situation if after all the fuss I had created the course did not take place.

Then *Gay News*, a fortnightly newspaper for homosexuals, ran a story about the course in its issue number 79 and in the week before the course the co-ordinator wrote saying he had experienced a twinge of worry at seeing the date, time and precise venue of the course given in the story. He went on:

My reasons are these:
1 Will a load of people turn up, not realising one *enrols* for adult education courses and pays a fee?
2 Will there be a danger that too many people enrol?
  Rise above fifteen and a real dialogue is impossible.
3 Any dangers of zapping? It is now many months since I attended a public, or semi-public, meeting on homosexuality which did not have some zapping (to put it mildly)!!!

In order to understand the anxiety about zapping, it is necessary to understand the essential differences between the GLF and the CHE. The GLF was a movement rather than a structured organisation, and, in so far as it was possible to ascribe to it a single political philosophy, tended towards a far-left view of society, its members seeing the liberation of homosexuals as part of a broader struggle to liberate all those oppressed by the capitalist system. And if not all members of the GLF subscribed to this political overview, by identifying themselves with the movement they did at least subscribe to the politics of confrontation in their fight for homosexual rights. The CHE, on the other hand, was a constituted organisation, with elected office-bearers and a letterhead naming any number of public worthies as non-executive vice-presidents. It was affiliated to the National Council for Civil Liberties and was an organisation whose essential concern was for the freedom of the individual homosexual and the establishment of legal safeguards for that freedom. Both the chairman of the GLF education group and the course co-ordinator were prominent members of their respective organisations and had clashed on public rostra before now. It was not inconceivable that the GLF supporters would interpret Addison's abandonment of their man (who after all had first suggested a course on the subject and fought long and hard for it) as a gross snub and turn up in force to zap the man from CHE, thereby destroying the course and my career along with it.

But while I shared the course co-ordinator's anxiety that too many might turn up and that some of them might be hostile, I was equally worried that the opposite might happen. When a course had been suggested two years earlier, the issue of homosexual rights had been a live one. Now, while the issues had not gone away, public interest had abated; and it was just possible that no one would turn up at all. And if that were to happen, it would be useless pointing out to the authority that the dismal turnout was the result of their own delays coupled with the uninformative blurb we had been saddled with. I would be blamed, and taken to task for creating so much fuss over a course for which there was demonstrably no demand.

In the last few days before the course I drummed up support, speaking to friends and colleagues, explaining the bind I was in and that they were not to be put off by the course description. Some said they would attend, others that they could not, and one woman, a lesbian, said the description was an insult to gays and that she would not attend.

On the evening of the first meeting I went to the branch, a secondary girls school during the day, not knowing what to expect.

Chapter 27

The Course

The First Meeting

Seventeen people enrolled for the course on 'Homosexuality: Changing Attitudes' and there was no zapping, but the first meeting was far from trouble-free.

Usually in the special studies courses at Addison we aimed to introduce flexibility and encourage class autonomy only after several meetings had taken place. I would suggest to most tutors that the first two or three meetings be tightly organised and provide a lot of hard information. The idea was to hit 'em hard and at the same time, by adopting a fairly conventional approach, allow the students time to grow accustomed to being back in an educational setting. By the third or fourth meeting, perhaps, the tutor could begin offering alternative topics or approaches; and from there, depending on the subject or the group, the students would be encouraged to play an increasing role in organising the course themselves.

However, in planning this course, the co-ordinator and I quickly realised that if we were going to abide by the second paragraph of the course description then we would have to forego the input of hard information at the first meeting and approach the subject tentatively, asking the group for guidance. Neither of us liked this de-structured start, but we were stuck with it, and so the course co-ordinator opened the first meeting by presenting a short paper setting out a number of topics—the traditional concept, the legal situation, gay women's liberation, the homophile movement, gay life-styles, befriending and counselling, homosexuality and the press—

then called for discussion on how we might examine them. Almost immediately we were in difficulties. People made suggestions that displayed their ignorance of the subject or that were impossible for us with our limited resources to pursue. One student suggested we abandon guest speakers altogether; and having just announced that the course design was in the hands of the group, the course co-ordinator had to retract, explaining that we were constrained by certain guidelines to make use of a pool of speakers. Not unreasonably, the student objected to this about-face. The course co-ordinator pulled the discussion together and steered it back to the paper, but it was an unhappy start from which the first evening never fully recovered.

But all was not lost. People had enrolled and expressed enthusiasm for the course. Several students from previous Addison courses had enrolled, and from the look of the rest there seemed every chance that a good study group would come together. And if nothing else, the meeting had demonstrated that a group of adults could gather together in a classroom and discuss homosexuality without causing outrage or bringing ILEA into disrepute.

This, however, did not appear to be the opinion of an observer from County Hall who had sat silently throughout the first meeting. The course met on a Wednesday and by Monday I had seen copies of a report of the meeting and an additional minute, addressed to the assistant education officer responsible for ILEA adult education and circulated to my principal and the chairman of Addison's governing body.

Taken together, the report and minute expressed five concerns about the course. The first was that it was the same as the course Addison had previously proposed, and the same as the one proposed earlier by the South London GLF.

The second concern was about the composition of the group. The report suggested that the course was likely to be a discussion group set up by homosexual groups. The minute went further, saying that the group was composed largely, if not entirely, of homosexuals.

The third concern was to do with the motives of the students. The report judged that two of the group would try to introduce a balanced study but that the discussions were likely to be directed towards confirming homosexuals in their attitudes and gaining public acceptance for their views.

The fourth concern was that the course was unlikely to result in any real learning or critical inquiry into the subject. The report suggested that the course put public funds at the service of one-sided propaganda.

And the fifth concern was about publicity. The minute suggested that the course would receive a lot of publicity through the homosexuals, who would claim it as an example of their success in getting a group operating within the adult education service and as an indication of some measure of official recognition. The minute went on to say that it would be preferable to have the publicity of closing the course down.

The Second Meeting

I was most worried about the labelling of students as homosexual. Addison had set up and advertised the course in good faith; and I imagined the students in their turn had placed a certain trust in Addison not to categorise them in any particular way simply because they had chosen to attend. I wondered whether we should abandon the course. Then the principal announced that he would attend the second meeting as an observer and, with the prospect of a second opinion, the course co-ordinator and I decided to go ahead.

The co-ordinator opened the second meeting by asking course members to say something about themselves. They were a worker from an advice centre, a social worker, a property developer, a builder's labourer, a community worker, a health visitor, a student teacher, an art dealer, an adult education tutor, a further education lecturer, an audio-visual technician, an unemployed man, a retired man and a retired woman. Ages ranged from early twenties through middle age to the two people in their retirement. Although the course co-ordinator did not ask the students to state whether or not they were homosexual, everyone did so. Six said they were and eight said they were not. Two people came in late and did not give any information about themselves. There were sixteen students at that meeting, seven of whom were women and nine men. Despite my worries about the first meeting, only one person had dropped out.

The guest speaker, a midwife and active in her local CHE group, then spoke about society's response to the woman homosexual. She dealt with the subject generally first, then described an alleged case of discrimination relating to a professional training course. It was a case that had been taken up by the National Council for Civil Liberties, and the speaker used it to raise a number of issues. There was some discussion but by now the group realised they were under observation and for the most part the evening only limped along.

The principal wrote a report to the chairman of the institute's governing body, giving his views on the make-up of the group, their motives for attending, the learning content of the course, and the likely publicity the course might attract.[47] He arrived at conclusions somewhat different from those in the report and minute about the first meeting, and my hope was that now the course would be allowed to continue under reasonably ordinary conditions.

The Third Meeting
The speaker at the third meeting was a member of another branch of CHE. He showed a set of slides accompanied by a synchronised tape which had been put together by his group and with which they hoped to embark on a campaign of 'social education' in their area, showing it to rotary clubs, to trade union groups, and in colleges of further and higher education. The slide-tape gave certain statistics in relation to homosexuality, looked at the effects of discrimination, and put the case for the homosexual's right to as free an expression of his or her sexual and emotional life as the heterosexual.

The slide-tape and speaker occupied the first hour, during which both the principal and vice-principal were present as observers. At break the principal left. The vice-principal stayed for the second hour.

At the beginning of the second half there was a small but significant example of how the sense of being under scrutiny hampered the running of the course. The co-ordinator wanted to take up the central point of the slide-tape and discuss 'what is normal?'. He suggested that we split into buzz groups, but one person objected strongly. In any other course I would have encouraged the tutor to override the single objector, but in this course we were so fearful of the accusation of manipulating the students that we stayed as a single group for the rest of the evening.

Once again the discussion only limped along and it is likely that we would have had a third thoroughly unsatisfactory meeting had the vice-principal not left a quarter of an hour before the end. Almost as soon as he walked out of the room the discussion came alive. 'You could see everyone relax', one of the group said afterwards. The subject shifted to the problems of coming out — the courageous, often traumatic action on the part of the homosexual of openly announcing to his family, friends and colleagues that he is in fact a homosexual. Several homosexuals in the group talked of their own experiences, of the self-doubt, the fears of discovery, the self-repression before they came out, and of their decision to come out and its effect on themselves and those around them. The discussion flowed, with people exchanging opinions and searching out information and with the course co-ordinator feeding in facts to keep the discussion moving in a positive direction. At last a dialogue was established, at last what we had set the course up for was happening!

The Fourth and Fifth Meetings

For the fourth meeting the course co-ordinator presented a paper on homosexuality and the law, drawing on his experience in the field of civil liberties and his work in helping draft a private member's bill aimed at removing legislative anomalies concerning homosexuality. It was a good meeting.

At the fifth meeting a criminologist presented a paper on labelling theory and societal definitions of deviance. She had no connection with the homophile movement and I went to some pains to tell her about the dust clouds surrounding the course. She nevertheless agreed to speak and the discussion that followed her paper with its coldly professional use of words such as 'deviance' and 'abnormal' was long and heartfelt.

It is all too easy now to see that these two meetings came at the wrong time. In almost any other circumstances we would have started with a much more detailed introduction, then these two lectures, then have moved by way of the slide-tape to the case history, and on in whatever direction the group wanted to take. Certainly, in the form we adopted, the course was no educational showpiece.

The Final Meeting

For the first half of the final meeting I spoke on the background to the course. I did so because the story itself was a comment on the way institutions can still react to homosexuality; and because I felt obliged to explain to the group why they had been under such scrutiny. In the second hour the co-ordinator asked the students to comment on the value or otherwise of the course as a whole.

One of the men said he was homosexual. Although he was a member of his local CHE group, he had not come out at work. He had attended the course because he wanted to learn more about the attitudes of heterosexuals to homosexuality. He now realised that his idea of a heterosexual's attitude had been stereotyped, and he had since come out at his place of work.

A woman said she had attended out of general interest, that she could understand much better now why homosexuals saw themselves as a minority group with rights still to be won, and that as a result of the course she would be much more wary about fitting labels to people.

Another man echoed these views. He and his wife had come to the course because they had several friends who were homosexuals. The course had made him understand more clearly the anguish some of these friends went through.

A married woman said she always attended evening classes. She had chosen this one this year because she was interested in the problems of sexuality. She felt the course could have investigated much more deeply why our society lays such a stress on sex of whatever orientation.

And so on.

Most agreed that the course had left a great deal to be desired, but most also agreed with the woman who said that the drawbacks had been compensated for by the 'extraordinary range of students' who had attended.

After the meeting we went to the pub, where the badges three of the group were wearing drew several other drinkers into the conversation. On that evening at least it seemed that we would have attracted less opposition if we had held the course in the pub in the first place.

After the Shouting

And after the shouting had died down and the dust had settled, what had we proved? Quite clearly ILEA at the outset had wanted nothing to do with a course on homosexuality, but under pressure had been obliged to recognise the internal logic of a system based upon response to demand, and had gradually yielded. But the applicants had been obliged to temper the original proposal in the process, bowing to the authority of the academic board and the governing body of the institute and operating within conditions set by officers seeking to interpret central authority policy. The result was a course that did manage to put a homosexual point of view, but lacked the coherent structure and political edge of the original proposal. The crunch ended in compromise.

Had the two years of argument been worth it? As far as the course is concerned, some of the speakers and papers were good, but the discussions were rarely anything but stilted. There was no sense of progression from meeting to meeting. And were the people who responded to my last-minute pleas for support bona fide students? (At least five attended as a result of my personal recruitment in the week before the first meeting.) But not everyone shared my gloom. Midway through the course I saw one of the group at a course at another branch.

'I hope you'll be there tomorrow evening' I said.

'Why? Are you worried about numbers?'

'Yes, I am. I wouldn't be surprised if no one turned up.'

'I think the group's stronger than that' she said. 'You should hear the chat during tea break.'

Small comfort, but comfort nevertheless.

But I have no doubts about the value of the long-term results of the battle to get the course on. These were formalised in the report of the working party on *The Educational Approach to Controversial Learning Situations*, which was circulated to all ILEA institutes early in 1977. It is a short document, but it is worth reading because it recognises:

1 that 'experimentation and innovation is a part of any vital adult education programme' (para. 11);

2 that 'it is most appropriate that institutes should be positively involved in the consideration of matters of current concern' (para. 11);

3 that 'it is, of course, a well-established practice for a local or topical issue to be used as a stimulus to arouse the interest of the students' (para. 6);

4 that 'this active approach, this attempt to stimulate and encourage learning situations in the manner and place where they will best flourish, is a valid educational role for institutes to engage in' (para. 7);

5 that visiting lecturers from organisations holding a committed viewpoint 'have an important part to play in providing interest and "edge" within the total educational objectives of the course or class' (para. 5);

6 that 'it may, of course, be possible to appoint a tutor with the required expertise who whilst holding strong views on his subject is also capable of explaining other views in opposition to his own and of helping students to make up their own minds' (para. 9);

7 that 'the institute will even from time to time find itself engaged directly in action itself as an inevitable result of its own activities' (para. 7);

8 that 'the aim of any course, whether on a controversial issue or not, should be that of *challenge*, rather than of *reinforcement* of existing attitudes, or uncritical habits of mind' (para. 8).

As I read it, the report argues quite clearly that adult education has a role to play in the raising of people's social and political consciousness. It is no accident that the word 'objective' does not occur anywhere in the report's four and a quarter pages.

Chapter 28

Survival Learning in Action

Unemployment

In mid-1977 the number of unemployed people in Britain was officially just over 1.6 million. In the first half of 1978 the number had 'dropped' to 1.4 million.[48] The figures are already horrific but they still do not take into account the large number of people, particularly among the young, who are out of work but for a variety of reasons do not register; nor the women who would work if there were work available but are forced to remain dependent on their husbands' salaries; nor those men and women over retirement age who would prefer to go on working rather than draw a pension. If all these were included in our calculations, what would we do with the official figure? Double it?

Even then the statistics would only tell part of the story. When the breadwinner loses his or her job, the rest of the family suffers. Perhaps another two or three million are directly affected, while all of us are indirectly affected by the strains mass unemployment places on the public services, the standards and quality of life, the morale of the community at large.

And then there is the effect of being unemployed on the individual.

'Do you mind if I talk to you?'

I was handing out leaflets outside the unemployment benefits office. A woman had taken one and walked on, hesitated, and come back. 'No, of course not' I said.

'I've been out of work for four years' she said. 'It's a nightmare.' I went on handing out leaflets as she talked. She was a fashion buyer and her last job had been with a large department store. With the onset of hard times in the firm she had been made redundant, and she had not found another job. She had tried hard at first, but with each refusal had grown increasingly desperate. Slowly but surely she lost her contacts. Prospective employers began asking her why she had been out of work so long. She began having debilitating periods of depression. She avoided her friends, no longer able to face anyone who had a job or who was married to someone who had a job. She felt irrelevant. Now after four years she was actually afraid of finding a job. The prospect was too daunting. She doubted whether she had the mental or physical stamina to work a full day. She was afraid of the responsibility. The circle had closed: being unemployed had robbed her of the ability to work.

She spoke to me, a perfect stranger, for more than half an hour, pouring out her story and staring at me in dismay.

'I am in my fifties' she said. 'What hope have I got now?'

The Poor Cousin's Response

I am not going to suggest in some expansive, waffly way that adult education is the panacea to the ills of unemployment. Most people who are out of work want a job and the money that goes with it; and adult education does not have $1\frac{1}{2}$ million jobs to offer. Nor am I going to suggest that adult education crash in on the business of further education or vocational retraining. The colleges and government skill centres are there to do that. All I want to do is list a number of activities that adult education, resting firmly down at the 'non-vocational' (that is non-examination) end of the education spectrum, can provide and that might to some extent at least help people who are out of work.

Leisure learning. In a way adult education already provides a service for those who are out of work in the form of its regular leisure learning programmes. Of course, many will be too preoccupied with the search for work to undertake a regular activity and others will consider that what adult education has to offer is irrelevant to the central problem of their lives.

Offering 'Holiday French' to an out-of-work storeman may look like an insult. But for some an adult education activity may provide a lifeline, a brief distraction from depression, a productive break in an otherwise empty week. It may provide something as simple and essential as the company of fellow human beings engaged in a common endeavour, or it might introduce the unemployed adult to learning as a lifetime pursuit. And it is always possible that by engaging in a learning activity an out-of-work adult might develop a latent talent or be given the stimulus to strike out in a new direction.

Literacy tuition. Some people are out of work because they cannot read or write well enough. Adult education has recently played a major part in a nationwide scheme to combat adult illiteracy, and centres and agencies continue to provide classes and to sponsor one-to-one tuition schemes.

Classes in English as a second language. Some people cannot get jobs because they do not speak English well enough. Most adult education centres in areas where there is an immigrant population from non-English-speaking countries run a range of classes in English as a second language.

Numeracy tuition. Some people cannot get jobs, or are not accepted for retraining schemes, because they lack basic maths. Adult education centres can, and many do, provide classes in basic numeracy skills.

Co-operative workshops. During 1976 Cowley Recreational Institute in South London began encouraging young people who were out of work to attend their woodwork shops during the day. A group formed, and gradually developed into an informal co-operative, making and selling toys and small pieces of furniture. Any money made was used to pay for additional materials, so that the co-operative did not provide paid employment; but it did provide training in new skills, valuable work experience, and practice in marketing and management.

Courses offering information and advice for the unemployed. In July 1977 South Lambeth Institute ran an intensive week-long course, making use of lectures, discussions, practical exercises, role-play and individual counselling. The course provided information on the kinds of work available, retraining, basic and further education opportunities, benefits and entitlements; and instruction on how to apply for a job, how to present one's work record, how to conduct oneself at an interview, and how to sell one's skills and labour.

Training professionals and activists. Many centres run courses on welfare rights for local professionals and activists. As an extension of these courses, or as complete courses in themselves, adult education centres could provide specialised training aimed at equipping professionals and activists with information that would enable them to offer reliable 'first aid' advice to unemployed people they came into contact with in the course of their work or community activities.

Study groups and lecture series. Making use of expert speakers from the disciplines of political science, sociology and economics, adult education centres could run study groups and courses that would take a long, hard look at the reasons for large-scale unemployment and analyse the various possible solutions, in both national and local terms.

Information on how to become self-employed. For some people a possible solution to unemployment might be to employ themselves. Adult education centres could provide short courses on the challenges and dangers of becoming self-employed, and provide information on VAT, setting up a company, raising money, advertising, marketing, etc.

Support groups. Adult education centres could run non-directive support groups along the lines of the 'Out of Work?' meetings described in Chapter 15, offering unemployed people a chance to meet, pool information, combat the isolation forced on them by being out of work, and see whether in discussion they might be able to find an answer to some of their problems. There is no real way of knowing how these groups would develop. Some might become consciousness-raising groups in which people got to know themselves better by asking and being asked pertinent questions; while others might become *political* consciousness-raising groups in which people asked questions such as: 'Why can't we work?' 'Why can't we work in jobs we like?' 'Who controls work?' 'Why . . . ?'

Residential courses. During the 1930s an extraordinary innovator in adult education called Frank Milligan set up a residential adult education centre to enable unemployed men to retreat from their everyday environment for a period, and, through a combination of leisure-learning activities and discussions, look anew at themselves and at the social and political situation of which their unemployment was a part. Now in the 1970s there are over thirty residential adult education centres in the country whose major function is to take in groups of adults for three- or four-day intensive courses in conventional leisure learning subjects. There are also a number of other residential centres run by local education authorities to which local adult education agencies have some claim. All of these centres could give over some of their programmes to emulating and extending what Frank Milligan did during the thirties.[49]

Wonder and Exasperation
Early in 1977 I attended a conference of adult educators interested in exploring the various ways in which adult education could respond to the problem of unemployment. About forty of us spent a day together in the basement of a community centre in Covent Garden, hearing from people who were out of work, from officers in government employment and retraining services, and from adult educators, one of whom came for the express purpose of arguing that there was absolutely nothing adult education could do. Despite the assertions of this sceptic, a lot of ideas were tossed around during the day, some of which I have listed above; and a document entitled *A Waste of People*, carrying a number of papers by people who had attended the conference, was subsequently produced by the City Lit. Training Unit. It is a challenging document, marking the changes in thinking that have been going on in the adult education world in the 1970s. But it arouses in me a mixture of emotions. And the conference did also. Indeed I remember growing increasingly restless as the conference went on into the afternoon, particularly when people began recounting their own experiments and projects. And I sensed that several others there were overtaken by the same sort of mood. For me it was a mixture of wonder and exasperation: wonder at the variety of response adult education was capable of, and exasperation at the realisation that because adult education was the poor cousin our response would have to remain marginal.

Just Imagine

I was in the office of the head of the general studies department of a college of further education two months later. We
were discussing a joint project the college and Addison were
engaged in, and while we were parcelling out the load of tutor
hours required for the project, he asked me casually how many
full-time staff Addison had and how many part-time tutor
hours our central authority overlords permitted us to spend in
a year. I told him that if one counted everyone, up to and
including the principal, we had nine full-time staff, that two of
those were full-time teaching staff, and that we were permitted
30,000 part-time tutor hours per year. He looked at me for a
while and then said: 'I have *fifty* full-time teaching staff under
me and can spend 11,000 part-time tutor hours over and above
that, and that's just one department!'

The disparity is sickening.

Just imagine what the poor cousin could do! Imagine what
an exciting, challenging, truly extraordinary *educational*[50]
service we could provide for the unemployed, the employed, the
young, the old, the handicapped, the disadvantaged, the
thoroughly privileged, this socio-economic class and that, if we
had a fair share of the educational budget.

Sit back for a moment, and imagine . . .

Notes

Notes

1 *Adult Education: A Plan for Development* (HMSO, 1973). Popularly known as the *Russell Report*, this document was much maligned when it first appeared as being all things to all men, and for not making strong enough proposals. It is nevertheless a thoroughgoing and perceptive description of adult education in England and Wales; and from time to time demonstrates character and bite—as in the section under the heading 'Government Lead' (paragraphs 155 - 60), from which my comments are taken.

2 The *Russell Report* puts 'the estimated expenditure on adult education' at 'about 1.1% overall of the total expenditure by local education authorities on all services' (appendix B, para. 24) but warns that the figures are approximations based on incomplete evidence. All this was for 1968 - 9. On ringing the Department of Education and Science in late 1977 I was told that 1.1 per cent was still used as a working figure and that more accurate figures were not available. It is a mark of how poor adult education is that no one seems sure of exactly how little is spent on it!

3 *ILEA Report 493* (1976). Even here the percentages are prefaced with the words 'about' or 'estimated as'.

4 For the most part in this book I use the general terms 'adult education centre' or 'adult education agency'. For a description of the various providers of adult education and the ways in which they differ from one another see the *Russell Report*, paras 81 - 124.

5 The account is by Victoria Radin in the *Times* Diary on 9 August 1976.

6 This does happen. Adult education is not always free from the phenomenon that Tyrrell Burgess in *Education After School* (Gollancz, 1977) notes occurring in technical and further education colleges and which he describes as 'academic drift'.

7 See Jennifer Rogers and Brian Groombridge, *Right to Learn* (Arrow, 1976). In Chapter 7, 'Image, Publicity and Public Relations', they give detailed examples of the poverty and inappropriateness of many adult education prospectuses, and examples of adult educators' propensity for offputting formalese in their publicity.

8 I choose this point to mention Jennifer Rogers, *Adults Learning* (Penguin, 1971). It is an excellent book, making copious use of verbatim comment from tutors and students. I have not described classroom situations in the way Jennifer Rogers does, so recommend her book as a useful foil to some of the 'extreme' situations and 'unusual' courses I shall describe now and later on.

9 Here again the figure is only an estimate and relates to 1968-9.

10 I am in danger of making this sound too easy. Adult education *can* make use of the professional (and the horse's mouth and the passionate amateur) but some adult educators, caught in Tyrrell Burgess's academic drift, tend to ignore the wealth of human resource in their communities and look to the other sectors of the education service first in their search for tutors.

11 The *Russell Report*, table 3, page 204. Again this is for 1968-9. In my phone conversation with the DES I was told (after the standard warning that 'it all depends on how you define an adult education student') that the figure had risen in the mid-1970s to nearly 3 million and that it had dropped to approximately 2½ million for 76-7. It is to be hoped that this lack of any real statistical base for understanding adult education will be corrected in time. In 1977 the Education Secretary set up the Advisory Council for Adult and Continuing Education, and this body has taken as one of its top priorities to investigate how the necessary statistics can be gathered.

12 In this chapter, for simplicity's sake, I talk of the adult educator as a full-time head of centre. But full-time heads of department, part-time heads, part-time tutors in charge of branches—indeed any *organiser* of adult education activities—will need some at least of the following skills and qualities.

13 In *Planning Local Adult Education Provision*, by Frank Youngman (Frobisher Resource Centre, 1975) there is a final section by the principal, Jim Anders, in which he outlines in diagrammatical form the organisational framework of Frobisher Institute and describes how he has tried to maintain optimum flexibility within a manageable structure.

14 A remarkable example of the indifference of politicians to adult education is to be found in the joint report of the ILEA schools sub-committee and the further and higher education sub-committee on 'Multi-Ethnic Education' (November 1977). Certain institutes had been running ethnic group studies for years, providing a wide range of language classes for immigrants, and running mother-tongue classes. Yet in the section headed 'Present practice within the Authority', the report makes no mention of adult education at all!

15 This letter appeared in *ILEA Contact*, 3 February 1978, from two teacher-governors of a large London comprehensive school:

> We feel our school buildings are over-used by adult evening classes to the detriment of our school community life. The next meeting of our governing body will consider the use of the school after 4.30 p.m. We would be very interested to hear from colleagues in other schools who have experience of the extended day, attached youth clubs or other arrangements whereby pupils *rather than evening class students* can benefit from facilities available.

The italics are mine. One wonders at the two teachers' concept of community.

16 The family workshop movement in adult education is a fascinating and important one. I have not pursued it in this book because I have only a limited personal experience of it. Mike Cutts, one of the originators of the Allfarthing Workshop, writes about the workshop and some of the thinking that has come out of the experience in *Adult Education*, Vol. 47, No. 5 (1975). The implications of the family workshop go far beyond a day of play and leisure. Towards the end of his article Mike Cutts says: 'Every person is different and learning environments have to be created by people who comprise societies rather than by those who desire power over societies'. Thus the family workshop can be related directly to some of the political issues discussed later in the book. This is brought out in some detail in a social/political evaluation of Allfarthing by David Head in *There's no politics here* (at the City Lit. Training Unit, 1977). |

17 Where adult education in Britain began is a matter of choice. Thomas Kelly begins his *A History of Adult Education in Great Britain* (Liverpool University Press, 1962) in the Middle Ages. Most commentators would probably more realistically locate the beginnings of the modern movement in the last century. But I like the starting-point taken by Robert Peers in *Adult Education — A Comparative Study* (Routledge & Kegan Paul, 1958). He locates the beginnings of adult education in the Methodist movement in the eighteenth century, saying: 'The Methodist class meeting . . . became a living focus for discussion and provided the model for much of the voluntary educational activity which was to be so characteristic of the working class movement of the following century' (p. 6).

18 John Ward and Stuart Weir. Stuart Weir writes an account of the course at Hoxton Hall in *WEA News*, September 1971, referring to the 'breakneck speed' with which it was set up within the institute's programme. Such was the novelty of the course and the apparently radical nature of its content that *WEA News* felt impelled at the end of Stuart Weir's article to state that the article 'expresses his personal views only'.

19 See Tony Palmer's *The Trials of Oz* (Blond and Briggs, 1971). It is a fascinating account of the trial and through the testimony of the defence witnesses becomes a description of many of the changes in ideas and social behaviour that took place in the 1960s.

20 A summary of these results and a commentary on them can be found in the cumbersomely titled *Report by the working party on the social structure of the student body of adult education institutes* (ILEA, 1973).

21 Despatches from the front line:

Keith Jackson, 'Adult Education and Community Development', *Studies in Adult Education*, Vol. 2, No. 2 (1970).

Tom Lovett, 'EPAs — an interim report', *Adult Education*, Vol. 43, No. 5 (1971).

Tom Lovett, 'Community Adult Education', *Studies in Adult Education*, Vol. 3, No. 1 (1971).

Keith Jackson and Tom Lovett, 'Universities and the WEA — an alternative approach', *Adult Education*, Vol. 44, No. 2 (1971).

Keith Jackson, 'Community Adult Education—the role of the professsional', *Adult Education*, Vol. 44, No. 3 (1971).

22 Keith Jackson and Tom Lovett, 'Universities and the WEA—an alternative approach', *Adult Education*, Vol. 44, No. 2 (1971).

23 John Brown. His support of the welfare rights course at Bethnal Green and his application for an outreach worker are significant moments in ILEA adult education.

24 The action research worker referred to is Stephen Parrott. Despite severely limited resources, he has managed to bring successful university provision to two large London estates, and on the White City estate in particular has prepared the ground for tenants' groups and a number of agencies (Addison Institute included) to engage successfully in educational activities and social action.

25 I insisted here that the class be open to all, and I still believe very strongly that this is right. But I do recognise that there can be cases where exclusive classes—open only to members of an already clearly defined group—might be justified as a preliminary step to an open class or as part of a crash programme to bring a defined group up to par, in language skills, say, with the rest of the community.

26 There is an account of what led up to this course by David Head, the other outreach worker, in Chapter 5 of *Growing Persons* (British Council of Churches, 1977); and a detailed account of the course itself, again by David Head, entitled 'Off-work, off-leisure' in *Adult Education* Vol. 48, No. 5 (1976).

27 The BBC has played a major role in developing methods of teaching languages to adults. Its radio and TV language series in the early and mid-1970s have been ever more inventive and it has maintained a consistently high standard in the published material accompanying its programmes.

28 Swami Prem Agamar (Derek Cunningham). He has not written about his programme at Central Wandsworth but his work has influenced the programmes of two other London institutes directly (and several others indirectly), and has enriched the lives of a large number of people.

29 Bertolt Brecht sees learning as a political act in a poem 'In Praise of Learning' quoted in *The Politics of Literacy* (edited by Martin Hoyles, Writers and Readers Publishing Cooperative, 1977). This is the second stanza:

> Learn, man in the mad-house!
> Learn, man in the prison!
> Learn, woman in the kitchen!
> Learn, sixty year old!
> You must take over the leadership.
> Search out the school, you homeless.
> Secure yourselves Knowledge, you who are frozen!
> You who are starving, grab hold of the book: it's a weapon!
> You must take over the leadership.

30 A remarkable example of this confusion of need with demand is recorded
by Peter Clyne in *The Disadvantaged Adult* (Longman, 1972). He describes the work of an adult educator in St. Paul's, a multi-ethnic, deprived
area of Bristol:

> On the basis of these identified needs a programme of social and edu-
> cational work was initiated in June 1970. All statutory and voluntary
> social workers were invited to attend a one-day conference on the subject
> of Young Jamaicans in Britain; 150 posters were displayed and 1,000
> leaflets were distributed. The conference was criticised and boycotted
> by many of the local Jamaican residents. However, more than fifty
> people attended. . . . (p. 110).

Despite opposition from the very people who were the subject of the
conference, they went ahead!

31 Pride in Addison and respect for my colleagues' work oblige me to say
that by 1977 Addison was providing on the White City estate an all-day
family workshop in a community hall, two keep-fit classes for women in a
nursery school, and a number of literacy and English for immigrants
classes in the community worker's flat, and was planning a joint institute
- university liberal studies programme.

32 Some adult educators go far beyond this and see adult education taking
up a central role. Peter Clyne in *The Disadvantaged Adult* (Longman,
1972) says that 'it is generally accepted, in theory if not always in
practice, that the peculiarly undefined and unstructured state of adult
education enables it to act as a bridge between the services of voluntary
and statutory bodies and different departments of local government.
Indeed adult education should be recognised as a crucial co-ordinating
community service'. (p. 3).
Tom Lovett in 'Community Development—a network approach', *Adult
Education*, Vol. 46, No. 3 (1973) draws a diagram representing community agencies, services and groups; and places adult education at the
centre. Both writers impose optimistic roles on a marginal service and are
in danger of robbing adult education of the ability to chase around on
the sidelines, nagging at the services and helping people ask uncomfortable questions.

33 David Head has written a detailed account of his experiences with this
group in 'Education at the Bottom', *Studies in Adult Education*, Vol. 9,
No. 2 (1977).

34 For the judiciary, see J. A. G. Griffiths, *The Politics of the Judiciary*
(Fontana, 1977).

35 Frank Youngman, *Planning Local Adult Education Provision* (Frobisher
Resource Centre, 1975).

36 Keith Jackson, 'The Marginality of Community Development—Implications for Adult Education' *International Review of Community Development* (1973).

37 Tom Lovett, *Adult Education, Community Development and the Working Class* (Ward Lock, 1975).

38 Tom Lovett, 'EPAs — an interim report' *Adult Education*, Vol. 43, No. 5 (1971).

39 The defenders of an adult education service for 'everybody' — senior executives, trade unionists, women, the working class, immigrants etc., etc. — are Jennifer Rogers and Brian Groombridge in *Right to Learn* (Arrow, 1976). Their response to the Coventry proposals would probably be found on p. 110 of their book:

> But to spare money for those most in need, if it were to mean leaving the rest of society to its own devices, to random forms of self-help, to the caprices of the market, is in fact aristocratic, not democratic; philanthropy, not a policy for the common good.

40 As quoted by Frank Youngman in *Planning Local Adult Education Provision* (Frobisher Resource Centre, 1975). I have not seen the original circular but it is worth quoting because it seems to demonstrate, in its use of punctuation, the way additional groups were simply tacked on to the end of the list as they came to people's minds.

41 In fairness to Peter Clyne, he does warn against the dangers of using a blanket term like 'disadvantaged'; but his book, *The Disadvantaged Adult* (Longman, 1972), and the *Russell Report* between them have established the word as a blanket term in adult education parlance.

42 A thumbnail rule might be: if the clients can refuse the provision there may still be room for *education*, but if they are under such constraints that they cannot refuse, then what they are receiving is *treatment*.

43 In Part 3 of *The Disadvantaged Adult* (Longman, 1972) under the heading 'Adult education in culturally and socially poor communities' Peter Clyne gives a number of impressive examples of good adult education practice. But labels are fraught with dangers, and one needs to read this section of his book in the context of the arguments put forward in *Tinker, Tailor . . . The Myth of Cultural Deprivation*, edited and introduced by Nell Keddie (Penguin, 1973).

44 See Terence Jackson, 'A new look at parent education', *Adult Education*, Vol. 50, No. 5 (1978).

45 *Report by the working party on the social structure of the student body of adult education institutes* (ILEA; 1973), para. 99.

46 F. E. Kenyon in *Homosexuality* (a Family Doctor booklet, British Medical Association, 1973) estimates that one person in twenty-five of the adult male population and one in forty-five of the adult female population are homosexual. As he observes, this is a sizeable minority. Campaigning groups would consider his figures an underestimate. One in ten of the adult male population is a figure often suggested.

47 To the best of my knowledge, the only publicity generated by the course consisted of a story in *Gay News* and a story in the *West London Observer*, both short pieces on inside pages and both published before the course took place.

48 The drop in the official figures may be unreal since over the past three years an increasing number of people have been taken off the

unemployment register by government work experience and job creation schemes. These special measures and subsidies were reported in the *Guardian*, 22 March 1978, to be keeping an estimated 250,000 people out of the dole queue.

49 See Brian Groombridge, 'The Wincham Experiment—Frank Milligan and the Unemployed', *Studies in Adult Education*, Vol. 8, No. 2 (1976).

50 I leave the last word in the notes to Sidney Heaven, an inspector with a long career in further and adult education. In a paper, 'Viewpoints and Issues in Community Education', which he spoke to at the Community Education Seminar at Goldsmiths College, 1977, he said:

I see useful distinctions to be drawn between upbringing, schooling, training, instruction, and education. I do not apply the word 'education' to the process of preparation for adult status: I think that education is something which only truly begins when adult status has been attained.